HERDER

MODERN LANGUAGE STUDIES

General Editors:
PROFESSORS J. BOYD, A. EWERT, AND W. J. ENTWISTLE

HERDER

Portrait by Gerhard von Kügelgen

MODERN LANGUAGE STUDIES

HERDER

A. GILLIES

PROFESSOR OF GERMAN LANGUAGE AND LITERATURE
IN THE UNIVERSITY OF LEEDS

BASIL BLACKWELL
OXFORD
1945

TO
MY WIFE

Printed in Great Britain for BASIL BLACKWELL & MOTT, LIMITED
by A. R. MOWBRAY & CO. LIMITED, London and Oxford

PREFACE

HERDER is known to students of German literature as the teacher of Goethe and the fountain-head of German Romanticism. He was also a major force in the national uprising of the Slav world. Detailed study, extending over many years, has convinced me that he is more than that. His function seems to me to be the counterpart of that of Kant, his great opponent, in the making of the mind of modern Germany. He formulated its emotional content, as Kant formulated its intellectual content; he taught it the self-conscious cultivation of universality, and created for it a modern variety of Mysticism. He presented it with a faith of uncommon dynamic power, if also of peculiar indistinctness, which has led to many subsequent perplexities, as it has taken effect, perplexities as disconcerting to Germany as to the outside world. Herder's appeal is thus more than a merely literary one. A theologian, educator, historian, and philosopher, his message is of the widest application. The warmth and depth of his personality can still be felt to-day; the full-hearted enthusiasm of his nature—tireless despite its many disappointments and frustrations—communicates itself to us across the years.

This bi-centenary study owes much to the encouragement of friends and colleagues. I must especially record my obligation to Professor L. A. Willoughby, who years ago opened my eyes to Herder's importance; to Professor James Boyd, for much assistance in smoothing the path of publication; to Professor Victor Murray, for his genial interest; and above all to Dr. C. H. Hay, who inspired the book's completion, who twice read the manuscript, and whose patience, wisdom, and scholarship have been responsible for countless improvements.

A. G.

June, 1944

v

CONTENTS

The portrait of Herder forming the frontispiece was painted after Herder's death by Gerhard von Kügelgen in 1809. Caroline Herder considered it to be the best likeness of her husband.

The portrait facing page 114 is ascribed to Anton Graff and probably belongs to the year 1803.

HERDER

CHAPTER I

THE SCENE

THE foundation of the historical outlook has been described as one of the greatest intellectual revolutions of European thought and, next to the Reformation, the most significant contribution of the German mind.[1] Ever since the end of the eighteenth century it has grown and marked off Germany sharply from the nations of the West, in that she has developed this outlook more profoundly than they, although it has not remained her exclusive property. The generalizing mode of thought of Western nations, based upon the belief in a universal natural law and in the ideals of Ancient philosophy and Christian ethics, is faced in this new approach with an individualizing attitude that lays stress upon local and temporal circumstances. The new outlook thus denies the absolute validity of Western values. The proper study of mankind is no longer man in isolation, but man in all the conditions that determine his being. The oneness of man with nature is something more keenly and consciously felt by the Germans than by men of the Western countries. Their poetry and their music clearly reveal this.

The main source of this outlook in Germany is Herder. He created the mood, drew up the plans, and began the execution. Others, starting with Hegel and the Romantic writers, worked at the structure itself, adding, altering, and filling in detail. Herder's predecessors in this sphere were, in the main, as Renan saw, thinkers of the West; Shaftesbury, Montesquieu, and Hume being the chief. Their conclusions were transformed in his fertile mind, through contact with certain native factors. To them he added, on the one hand, the gradually emerging philosophy of Leibniz and, on the other, the age-long yearnings of Mysticism. The feeling of dependence upon the universe and of oneness with God—the native piety of the German soul that Schleiermacher stressed—revealed itself in the Mysticism that still lived on in eighteenth-century East Prussia and formed the spiritual atmosphere of Herder's upbringing. A touch of Scholasti-

[1] F. Meinecke, *Die Entstehung des Historismus*, Munich, 1936, I. 1-2.

B

cism, that survived in academic theology—Herder's chosen field—and, at a later stage, a re-reading and adaptation of the philosophy of Spinoza completed the background. The outcome was something quite different from the Western attitude to history, something much less precise and less tangible, but, for this very reason, the more provocative in its consequences. Gibbon, the English heir of Hume, was a better historian than Herder, and his historical sense accordingly more sharply defined, but can it be said that his influence has affected the many departments of subsequent thought that Herder's has done? Has the English mind ever since been haunted by the exciting allurements of historical vistas and speculations—and mirages—, as the German mind has been since Herder, in its search for the self-assurance it has never attained?

It is not for nothing that Macaulay characterized the *Ideen* as an 'era in the intellectual history of modern Europe'.[1] Herder combined within himself the basic doctrines of Western thinkers with the inherently Romantic view-point of Germany. Subsequent German thought has tended to neglect the former and to overstress the latter, just as Western thought has done the reverse. Here is the key to that seemingly complete incompatibility of the German and the Franco-British standpoints in the modern world. Yet the two outlooks *are* in a way reconcilable, as Herder showed.

In its immediate application the historical trend meant nationalism, and Herder is correctly regarded as the father of modern nationalism. That discovery of the nation-state, of the hidden creative forces of the people, of the inevitable union of the individual with the national community, and of the determination of the present by the past— all this goes back to Herder. But he must not be censured for modern exaggerations. He fused these ideas with the Classical doctrines of common humanity and of the eternal natural law. Indeed, he made them subordinate to this, in that he regarded nationalism as the most significant stepping-stone towards internationalism, the foundation upon which all universal humanity must rest.

This was not the only result of his new approach. It meant also that existing sciences of all kinds received a fresh direction, and that new ones were initiated. The philosophy of history, psychology, linguistics, philology, the history of literature, biology, geography, pedagogy, archaeology, Biblical criticism, all the branches of knowledge, indeed, that throw light upon man's growth and his relation to his background, are in Herder's debt, in their meaning or sub-

[1] G. Trevelyan, *Life and Letters of Lord Macaulay*, 1877, I. 195.

stance. Nor, on the other hand, must the modern world forget his plea for the emancipation of women. His view was illimitable. Yet, in spite of this his destiny has been to be an influence on others rather than to stand out as a great individual figure. His reputation, as Goethe noted in 1828, has been largely anonymous. His *Ideen*, his greatest achievement, were no more in that year than 'ein vor fünfzig Jahren in Deutschland entsprungenes Werk, welches unglaublich auf die Bildung der Nation eingewirkt hat und nun, da es seine Schuldigkeit getan, so gut wie vergessen ist'.[1] In his lifetime he was overshadowed by his more distinguished contemporaries and he remained in eclipse until modern criticism, which he did so much to found, gradually began to discover that he meant far more than has been commonly fancied.

The historical sense was prepared by Herder's predecessors. The reason, however, why it asserted itself so strikingly in his work is ultimately to be found in the fact that contemporary circumstances, still under the inconceivably disastrous shadow of the Thirty Years' War, were so utterly unsatisfying and were so keenly resented as such by him. It is the outcome and at once became the further cause of that everlasting yearning that has dominated German thought, that sense of loss and inferiority, that introspection and longing, that *Sehnsucht* for something that is not. The West does not know these things in anything like the same degree. In Herder they are discernible from the beginning. He condemns his own age for its deficiencies, he looks back regretfully at what once was and indulges in visions of the might-have-beens of history. Then he pulls himself up and with hope that is tinged with melancholy feels bound to accept the course of things. At one and the same time he gives way to the bitterest and most querulous *mal du siècle* and voices a wistful fatalism that possesses something of the stoical. There is a strange disunity and incoherence in all this. It has persisted in later developments.

Herder's remedy was to substitute feeling for intellect, and faith for reason, as the mainsprings of human action. He thereby merely brought to the fore that emotional cast that is typical of the German mind, as De Quincey noted. Modern German literature, which was born at about the same time as Herder, was thus irrevocably led into emotional, nostalgic channels from the very start.

From the start, too, German literature was made aware of the

---

[1] Goethe, *Werke*, Weimar edition, I. XLI (2), 345; 'A work that was produced fifty years ago in Germany, and has had an incredible effect upon the culture of the nation, and, now that it has discharged its duty, is as good as forgotten.'

antithesis between itself and Antiquity, then the universal model. It was made aware that it had a mission to fulfil. The opposition of Modern and Ancient, North and South, Romantic and Classic was presented to it in Herder's first major work, his *Fragmente*. Romanticism has been its characteristic, accompanying the whole of its course. The *Fragmente* declared that out of the decay of Roman civilization, the invasion of the Teutonic tribes, the Arabic influence, the effect of Christianity, and the rebirth of Classical learning, there arose a new, *modern* spirit that was entirely different from that of Ancient times, a spirit as symbolical of the modern age as the Classical spirit was of Antiquity. Herder was not quite so far advanced that he could, as Friedrich Schlegel did, straightaway set up the sharply defined antinomy of Classic and Romantic, although he nearly did so. He was too much of an historian, he was too occupied with recounting how things had come about, with tracing the evolution of human thought and of the human race generally from ancient to modern times. Lacking the necessary confidence to follow up his discovery, he deplored, almost in the same breath, the whole nature of the modern epoch; he regretted Germany's loss of its national character; he looked back with longing admiration at the greatness of Greece. In Herder *Weltschmerz* and history lived in an uneasy partnership.

Herder absorbed and developed much that he found in the achievements of other men. Movements were afoot within Rationalism itself that tended to weaken the acceptance of the universal validity of reason upon which Rationalism was founded. He grasped and merged them into a highly suggestive combination. In Bossuet he saw a method that had accounted for the course of historical events by means of an orthodox theological creed, which discerned the guiding hand of Providence at work preparing man for the religion of Christ. Apart from its obvious narrowness, this method used the doctrine of Providence to explain that from which the existence of Providence should be concluded. Herder followed Bossuet in this. Vico held the same view and used it to deepen the cyclical theory of history, which Antiquity and the Renaissance had enunciated; his resultant doctrine of the eternal rise and fall, decline and regeneration, in the universe being something not far removed from Goethe's *Stirb und werde*. He saw, as Herder did, that man must remain in ignorance of the purpose of Providence. Vico's influence was, however, limited and, though the points of kinship with Herder are numerous, Michelet's observation: 'Pour voir l'homme, Herder s'est placé dans la nature; Vico dans l'homme même, dans l'homme s'humanisant par la société',[1] aptly states the difference; for it is the influence of human rather than of natural environment that Vico stresses. Vico, further, had no sense of the greatness of creative personality; and finally, if his transcendentalism was in danger of becoming blended with immanence, he remained at bottom a follower of Bossuet. It is doubtful, too, if Vico was known to Herder except as a name which Hamann mentioned in 1777; Herder does not refer to him until 1797 and was possibly indebted to Goethe, who had become acquainted with the philosopher's works in Naples, for the real introduction.

Voltaire marked an important advance. Believing human nature to be uniformly the same everywhere and at all times, he rejected the idea of the existence of a divine plan in history and proceeded to relate events to human mental processes, which he weighed in the scales of reason. He measured all things by the present; he condemned everything that was out of keeping with the tenets of Enlightenment, such as superstition, credulity, and unreason, though he was bound to admit the force of these irrational factors in the shaping of human affairs. Since history was thus used to show the evolution of Enlightenment, it followed that any alternative ideal would have to be similarly justified on historical grounds. Henceforth, histories were no longer to be mere compilations, and, inasmuch as Voltaire destroyed the traditional Christian interpretation of events, their scope was immensely widened, so as to embrace the non-Christian peoples of the world.

Rousseau, who inverted Voltaire's findings, cast doubts upon the worth of the present, thus attracting attention even more forcibly than ever to the idea of change and development in human affairs. Montesquieu, on the other hand, who was deficient in an appreciation of growth and evolution, examined the physical influences of environment upon man and his institutions, and believed that each nation and each epoch had a spirit of its own according to its geographical circumstances and mental structure. This really meant that human nature could not be universally the same; but Montesquieu, as a Rationalist, refused to accept the results of his own determinism. He still held to fundamental principles of ethics and common humanity. Herder was well aware of the weaknesses of the *Esprit des lois*.

Buffon's work turned away from this merely mechanical approach to a more vitalistic one and, while not historical, nevertheless affected the growth of Herder's outlook. At the same time Hume, in many

[1] Michelet, *Introduction à l'histoire universelle*, final *éclaircissement*.

ways in line with Voltaire, and believing like his age in the constancy of human nature and in the development of mankind from barbarism to culture, saw that there were certain things, certain 'secret causes', that reason could not explain. He concerned himself with the psychology of the human soul, though without fully realizing that this involved the study of individual phenomena. Further, his theory of causation asserted that there is no *a priori* connection of events; causation being no more than the inference drawn by the human mind from what experience shows to be the customary succession of events. This point had a great effect upon Herder, who mistakenly decided that the way was opened to conjecture, theory, divination, even fancy; and he indulged his native genius in this direction to the fullest extent.

To these results are to be added the effect of the Neo-Platonism of Shaftesbury and Leibniz. Both these men took account of variety and individuality everywhere; they saw life as something that is always changing, always renewing itself, and always possessing a relationship to other life. All things, Shaftesbury believed, come from God; all, whether good or bad, are comprehended within the great and beautiful harmony of the universe. He rejected the normative attitude of his age, but any real progress towards the historical outlook was prevented by his belief in perfectibility. Leibniz, whose rediscovery began in 1765 with the publication of his *Nouveaux Essais*, like Shaftesbury regarded each individual phenomenon as a mirror of the divine, containing the laws of its own being within itself and reflecting the eternal with different degrees of clarity. Leibniz drew attention to the unconscious and irrational side of man's being, declaring that not only reason but instinct too leads man towards the truth. Although he thus began to undermine the generalizing approach of the Enlightenment, Leibniz nevertheless accepted eternal verities as axiomatic, and spoke of progress, through a series of gradations of being, to ever higher and purer spheres of reason and perfection.

The Neo-Platonist contribution was, then, a major one. Its effect was at once seen in the work of Justus Möser (1720-94), the author of the *Osnabrückische Geschichte* (1768), whom Herder greatly admired. Here was a man who made an intensive study of a very special subject, dealing with mankind in real circumstances and not with generalities. Möser objected to the universal applicability of the principles of the Enlightenment. Each individual phenomenon must live according to its own rule, its *Lokalvernunft* (Bodin's *locorum ac regionum ratio*). He emphasized the vital importance of *milieu*, and recognized, as Shaftesbury and Leibniz and Hegel did, the existence of a divine rationality behind all variety. Like Montesquieu he saw that each nation and each epoch has its own character, and he divided up his history accordingly. A patriotic yearning for the native past is evident in Möser, but he lacked the great historical passion of Herder.

If the Enlightenment and Neo-Platonism formed two pillars of Herder's history, Pietism provided the third. This latter had expressed itself already in the *Unparteiische Kirchen- und Ketzergeschichte* (1699-1700) of Gottfried Arnold (1666-1714), a work that was written in direct contradiction to the intellectualist approach to history. Pietism proclaimed the absolute value, not of reason, but of the divine illumination of the soul. It was essentially a continuation of medieval Mysticism. Its doctrines were transmitted to Herder in his home atmosphere and later in the teachings of Hamann. He read widely in the literature of Mysticism; Tauler, Paracelsus, Johann Arndt, Jakob Böhme, Arnold, Swedenborg, Bengel, he knew them all. There was restored in Herder a direct sense of the almighty presence of God in all things; this was needed at a critical time in the evolution of his historical philosophy. What is mistakenly called pantheism in him is no more than the uprising of Mysticism, the desire of the soul for union with God and for the enjoyment of His instruction.

In addition to these major currents, there were other—and varied—streams from which Herder drew. On every side, in the wake of Montesquieu, environmental causes were being stressed. Only Herder saw that these were not in themselves sufficient, and that the representation of the human instincts as the driving forces of life was required as well. The Scottish historians, Ferguson, Robertson, and Millar, dealt with the development of society and the material factors that shaped it. The Abbé Dubos had already emphasized the favouring of poetic genius by a suitable environment. The British scholars Blackwell and Wood had declared that it was necessary to transfer oneself in spirit into the *milieu* of Homer if one were to understand him, and Lowth had made the same requirement in regard to the study of Biblical poetry. All these were in line with Montesquieu's view. Hurd's *Letters on Chivalry* (1762) went a stage further and asserted that the Middle Ages formed a far more favourable period for poetic production than Classical times, and that Shakespeare was their outcome. Lessing drew attention to national differences between German and French literatures. Winckelmann considered the evolution of Greek greatness out of local and temporal circumstances, but, inasmuch as he idealized the Greeks, he merely set up new norms for old. Young's demand for emulation rather than imitation implied that no one individual phenomenon should mould itself by another. The points raised were varied, and Herder combined them into a programme of the widest importance. He brought to the melodies that others were haltingly playing a new depth and more striking contours and combined them into arresting harmonic and contrapuntal movements.

For all his wide range, Herder belonged primarily to the field of literature. Poetry was the beginning and the end of all his effort. He studied it from every angle, delved into its sources of production, assessed its value and its influence as the expression of life, and weighed it as evidence concerning humanity at all times and in all places. He was the creator of the art of history of literature, as it is understood to-day. It is difficult to realize now that, when he began to write, his first task was to assure his country that it could have a poetic literature, even a language suitable for literature, at all. The extent of his influence is best appreciated when it is remembered that within his lifetime German letters assumed the leadership of the whole world.

The German language was Herder's first concern. He examined it carefully and with bitterness declared it to be a 'neumodisches Gebäude, das, mit fremden Zierraten überladen, bei seiner Größe klein und unansehnlich ins Auge fällt'.[1] Latin was still to a large extent the language of scholarship, and French that of culture. The French atmosphere of the court of Frederick the Great, as well as of other monarchs, is too well known to need emphasis. So many French words had been imported into Germany that the language was in danger, not of becoming a hybrid, but of becoming a *patois* spoken only by the uneducated classes. To be sure, the philosopher Wolff had created a German philosophical language, the poet Klopstock had introduced new emotional expressions, while Lessing had created an acute and lucid vehicle for critical and dramatic work. But the battle was not won; the whole front had not yet moved forward; only a few outer bastions had been carried. Herder reviewed the whole position, discovered incredible weakness, and decided how it could be remedied.

At the same time, too, he raised his voice in favour of originality in literature. Gottsched's reforms in the light of French practice were ambiguous achievements, for purification from appalling crudities was gained only at the cost of intolerable loss of liberty.

---

[1] Herder, *Werke*, I. 376. (All references are made to the standard edition of Herder's works by B. Suphan, Berlin, 1877-1913, the spelling being modernized); 'A new-fangled structure, which, overloaded as it is with foreign ornaments, strikes us as small and unimpressive, for all its size.'

This writer's immediate opponents, the Swiss critics Bodmer and Breitinger, stressed imagination and feeling rather than reason as literary forces and paved the way for Klopstock's *Messias* and *Odes*. It was an age of beginnings. In another direction Gessner, following the tradition of the preceding century, wrote idylls that swept across Europe. Gellert, the moral philosopher, was famous as a fabulist and as the importer of the Richardsonian novel and the *comédie larmoyante* into Germany, while Wieland was known mainly as the translator of Shakespeare and as the author of frivolous poems and of *Bildungsromane*. The dominating figure was, however, that of Lessing, supported by his friends Nicolai and Mendelssohn. The *Briefe, die neueste Litteratur betreffend* (1759-65) had just ceased to appear when Herder entered the field. Lessing had made his name not only as a redoubtable critic, but also as a leading dramatist and as the author of the *Laokoon*. Nicolai was an important personality in journalism, while Mendelssohn was probing deeply into new spheres in philosophy. Yet all the time, Germany was chained to foreign literary patterns.

When Herder's authorship commenced, there was need for outspoken challenge and inspiring guidance. He provided both. The whole world of literature was his to make. Apart from Lessing, he had no predecessors of note in the field of criticism in Germany. Like another Du Bellay (and there is much of the Renaissance in Herder), he assessed the value of his native tongue and pointed out its mission. He declared war on imitation. He evolved the ideas of the nation, the *Volk*, of creative personality, and of historical continuity. But, charging as he did his age with degeneracy, he initiated a crisis in German thought that has persisted unsolved. He brought *Sehnsucht*, *Weltschmerz*, emotionalism, irrationalism, Romanticism into the very forefront of all German effort. The attempt to reconcile yearnings with realities constantly occupied Herder, as it has occupied his country ever since. It is a far cry from the hard-headed rationalism of Lessing to the Romantic fusion of dream and reality, to Tieck's nostalgic cry:

> Mondbeglänzte Zaubernacht,
> Die den Sinn gefangen hält,
> Wundervolle Märchenwelt,
> Steig auf in der alten Pracht.[1]

It was Herder who bridged the gap.

[1] 'Magic night of moonlight, which holds the senses enthralled, wonderful world of fairyland, rise again in all your splendour.'

CHAPTER II

THE MAN AND HIS WORK

JOHANN Gottfried Herder was born on the 25th August, 1744, in the little East Prussian town of Mohrungen. The atmosphere of his home was one of piety, even solemnity. He was brought up on the Bible and the Lutheran prayer-book and from them he learned his first lessons in poetic appreciation. At no time were literature and religion separated in his mind.

From the first, Herder was unusually timid and impressionable. As a child he sensed hostility in the world and roamed the countryside to be away from the cheerless poverty of his surroundings. He attended a school kept by one appropriately named Grim, who spared his pupils neither the rod nor the intricacies of Latin grammar, and enlivened an arid curriculum only with the rudiments of Greek, Hebrew, and music. Much in Herder's ideals of educational reform sprang directly from his weariness of the repression he experienced. Yet Grim's bleakness and rigidity did not turn the boy from the pleasures of study and literature. Already there stirred within him the impulse to get beyond the narrowness of everyday life, even beyond the cramping bounds of reality itself. Books, nature, and his imagination were the springs on which he drew. And he drew liberally.

Herder's astonishing powers of assimilation found wide scope when he entered the house of a certain Sebastian Friedrich Trescho, an irritable hypochondriac, who was appointed minister at the Mohrungen church in 1760, and who gave the boy free lodging in return for his services as a copyist. Though the change was scarcely an improvement, and though his treatment by Trescho appeared tyrannical and degrading to Herder, especially in the resentment of later years, he at least obtained a unique privilege—the use of the minister's extensive library. He seized the opportunity with alacrity, for here was a new means of escape from an increasingly unsympathetic world. Solitude threw him more and more upon himself; the more he read—and his reading ranged from the Classics and theology to modern German literature—the more he became a creature of fancy. The sombre colour of his life became quite ineradicable. His first attempt at literature was symbolically entitled 'Gesang an den Cyrus von einem gefangenen Israeliten', an ode to Peter III of Russia; it was slipped by Herder into a parcel of manuscripts which Trescho sent to Kanter, the Königsberg bookseller and publisher, was printed and aroused some admiration.

The arrival of a Russian army-surgeon, Schwarz-Erla, in the winter of 1762 on his way back from the Seven Years' War, was a source of fresh hope. The newcomer was attracted to Herder and offered to take him to Königsberg, teach him surgery and cure him of the eye-trouble from which he had suffered since his fifth year. Herder, on his part, was to translate a medical treatise of the doctor's into Latin. Herder accepted the invitation, but his unfitness for the study of medicine was quickly apparent, and once more he was thrust back upon himself. Thereupon he took a courageous and momentous step. Without money in his pocket, in a strange town, against Schwarz-Erla's will and without his parents' consent, he registered as a student of theology on the 10th August, 1762, at Königsberg University.

The years in Königsberg shaped the course of Herder's career. Firstly, in return for free lodging, he became an assistant teacher in the Collegium Fredericianum, where his progress was so rapid that before he was twenty he was entrusted with the work of the upper school. It is true that he shed much of his shyness and angularity, but the gain was offset by an unnatural precocity that supervened. It was an unwise step to teach while he was still learning and before he had reached maturity. Secondly, in the bookshop of Kanter, to whom his ode to Cyrus had given access, he regularly met the leading scholars of the town, when they came in to look over the latest books. Here was an excellent opportunity to play the attentive listener and bring his knowledge of European literature up to date. Thirdly, he gained the friendship of two important men, who affected him incalculably.

Within a fortnight of registration Herder had become an enthusiastic follower of the lectures of Kant, who generously granted him free admission to his classes. He was enraptured by his teacher's all-embracing vision no less than by his personality, and though in later years he was to expend much energy in an embittered and futile attempt to controvert Kant's findings, he nevertheless composed the most generous of tributes to his influence upon him. The philosopher, who was then thirty-eight, had just been fascinated by Rousseau's *Emile*. Dissatisfied with easy-going metaphysical dogmatism and convinced of the limitations of human reason, he sought in experience and observation a new and firmer foundation for philosophical speculation. He strove for a system which would rest upon an unshakable scientific basis and in which the moral consciousness of man would have an assured place. His method was that of analysis, and it was method, as much as anything else, that his students learned from him. He lectured on logic, metaphysics, astronomy, mathematics, and moral philosophy; but it was his classes on physical geography, in which he studied the effect of climatic and other geographical conditions on human development, that particularly appealed to Herder. If he was incapable of Kant's systematic exactitude, Herder learned to look at the universe in all its fullness and variety, and to pierce through appearances to the principles underlying them. The cheerfulness, wit, and unmistakable vitality of Kant's teaching were, moreover, a revelation to one who had known only dullness and pedantry. His delight knew no bounds, and personal contact, when the philosopher talked freely of his own researches, raised it to white-hot fervour. Herder's immaturity, however, was a great handicap, and doubtless it was this that rendered the words of his second teacher, Hamann, so alluring.

For, early in 1764, the rich enchantment of these studies was supplemented by the friendship of Johann Georg Hamann, a man fourteen years older than himself and well versed in European literature. From Hamann his dark broodings and shapeless dreams suddenly gained force and direction. Kant's emphasis on the value of experience was given fresh meaning by his friend's mystical glorification of the senses. In Hamann's personality there was a strange mixture of sensualism and pietism, and his oracular, 'sybilline' writings had earned for him the name of 'der Magus im Norden'. With startling urgency he pointed to the most elementary, purely sensual beginnings of human activity, as being closest to the divine forces of creation. He inveighed against the cult of knowledge in which his age was occupied and exclaimed that all that we know is that we know nothing. Logic and abstraction are hindrances in the search for truth —'Durch den Baum der Erkenntnis werden wir der Frucht des Lebens beraubt'.[1] The true sources of knowledge are religious faith and the experiences of the senses—'Optimus maximus verlangt von uns keine Kopfschmerzen, sondern Pulsschläge'[2]—for the outward splendour of things, the world, nature, history, is a living manifestation of the divine, and God reveals Himself to the soul that believes and to the senses that feel. Hamann taught Herder to have eyes to see and ears to hear. Poetry was similarly explained by Hamann as revelation, springing from impulse and emotion, those hallowed channels

[1] 'By the tree of knowledge we are robbed of the fruit of life.'
[2] 'Optimus maximus (i.e. God) requires of us not headaches but pulse-beats.'

through which God reaches man and man reaches God; it is the mother-tongue of the human race, and poetic genius is a heaven-sent teacher through whom God speaks. In face of such a religious attitude as this, man-made rules of poetic composition become quite meaningless.

Now it is clear that no teaching could so forcibly have supplemented Kant's insistence upon the limitations of reason as this, and it is equally clear that none could possibly have been more acceptable or influential at this stage in Herder's development. But the question at once arises as to whether or not Hamann's influence, tremendous as it undoubtedly was, did not bring an element of confusion into Herder's mind. Is it possible that, while Kant set Herder on the track to which he returned in the *Reisejournal* and which led finally to the *Ideen*, by introducing him to the works and methods of philosophers and firing his imagination, his attention was deflected by Hamann from the sphere of physiography to the realm of poetry and criticism, as containing the more obvious and immediate tasks to be discharged? Is this the source of that inner conflict that later caused Herder to leave Riga? Can it be that Hamann destroyed that belief in scientific method that Kant was trying to inculcate, and replaced it by alogical emotionalism? Did he undo the major part of Kant's work and encourage that fatal lack of system that hampered Herder to the very end of his days? There is a temptation to answer these questions in the affirmative, if with qualifications. We know how unhappily Hamann interfered with Herder's conception of the origin of language, and we know that Herder was to spend the rest of his life seeking to harmonize those conflicting aspects represented by Hamann and Kant. And though it would be more than unreasonable to call Hamann any other than Herder's guiding genius, it is not too much to say that he did not give without destroying, and that while he made Herder a critic, he prevented him from becoming a philosopher. This, however, was not apparent at the time. It was better for German literature that Herder *was* a critic.

Together the two friends enjoyed the study of primitive poetry. The Old Testament commended itself particularly to Hamann, on account of its divine content, its indisputable antiquity, and its consequent proximity to the forces of Creation. The foundation of Herder's critical method was soon laid. Hamann was his literary adviser, ever at his side, and Herder was an eager listener. It was Hamann, too, who taught him English, and in unforgettable hours they read *Hamlet* and *Paradise Lost*. The contagious teaching of

Hamann, as of Kant, aroused Herder to a fuller consciousness of what had previously been scarcely more than indistinct shadows.

II. RIGA

In 1764 Herder's reputation as a teacher earned him promotion to the Cathedral School at Riga. In the following year he was licensed to preach and in 1767 was ordained and appointed minister at two of the principal Riga churches. He declined an invitation to a post in St. Petersburg in 1767. The Riga years were perhaps the happiest of Herder's unhappy life. He was never idle, and his growing versatility had ample scope. He quickly became an effective and popular preacher. He moved freely in a cultured society and had many influential friends. It was in Riga that he first became alive to the meaning of patriotism, for the public spirit of the self-governing Hanseatic city was a revelation to one who had shrunk from the state-system of Frederick the Great. If the enthusiasm he felt was Russian in sympathy, he was not prevented from becoming a good German as well. His patriotism took the form of desiring to teach his countrymen new ideals of life and to point the way to a new conception of culture. Already he foresaw the destruction that was to overtake the brocaded artificiality of the age; and already he had begun his never-ending effort to dispel the shadow of doom by showing how the glittering vanities and elaborate pomposities that were so evident might be replaced by vital principles and genuine human purposes. His patriotism, therefore, found its most appropriate outlet in his ideal of popular education, as well as in his passion for the regeneration of German literature. But five years were to elapse before he could realize even the implications of his plans.

Herder's literary work had already begun in Königsberg in the form of newspaper articles and reviews written under Hamann's supervision. He was barely twenty-three when his first book, the famous *Fragmente über die neuere deutsche Litteratur*, appeared, anonymously, in 1767. In it he dealt with the most pressing literary problem of the day, that of originality, and quickly found that he had written one of the leading works of the age, despite the offence his strictures gave to the die-hard school. A second edition was soon drafted, partly printed, but not published. A memorial essay on Abbt, Lessing's successor in the *Litteraturbriefe* (*Über Thomas Abbts Schriften, der Torso von einem Denkmal*, 1768) and the *Kritische Wälder* (1769), so-called after Quintilian's definition of the word *sylvae*, continued the offensive. Just as the *Fragmente* had arisen out of scattered comments on the *Litteraturbriefe*, so the first *Wäldchen* was a supplement to the *Laokoon*, which Herder read with avidity. The book was timed to coincide with Lessing's attack on the Halle professor Klotz, the principal foe of the *Fragmente*, and the second and third *Wäldchen* consist of an angry philippic against him and his noisy but now-forgotten clique. Herder's excessive sensitivity caused him to take the ill-advised step of denying, publicly and even to his closest friends, the authorship of the *Fragmente* and *Wälder*, though all the world knew the truth. A fourth *Wäldchen*, planned early in 1769, was recast after Herder's journey to France, but never published in his lifetime.

The Riga years were full of plans and preparations, of which only Herder's notebooks reveal the real extent. They soon became so pressing as to precipitate his departure. Indeed, in May, 1769, Herder astounded the city by resigning office and taking ship for France. It was a bold stroke and it finally settled his destiny.

The last straw was undoubtedly the unpleasant position into which his quarrel with Klotz had thrust him. The violence of his attacks, with his obstinate denials that he was the author of his own works, scarcely harmonized with his pastoral calling. His frantic efforts to preserve his dignity only led to further loss of it and he was soon quite unable to brace himself against the consequences of his evasiveness. A serious illness, moreover, had left his energy impaired. Then, in his sermons, he had consistently avoided dogmatic teaching, and this, at first regarded as a cardinal merit, aroused suspicions as to his orthodoxy when it became known that he had been admitted to a masonic lodge. On his part, Herder felt stifled in a position of dependence and yearned to address a wider public.

The real and fundamental cause of the breach, however, lay in the peculiar cast of his personality. There is a strange fitfulness about all his actions and decisions. He was the plaything of impressions and was never strong enough consistently to take the moulding of his life fully into his own hands. The fatalism that showed itself in later years was already at work. He believed in his genius with something approaching superstition, and the contrast between his projects and achievements became daily more distressing. His impotence exasperated his self-respect and revolted his pride. He had to choose. On the one hand lay continued submission, with the insincerities and agonizing self-reproaches that would certainly accompany it; on the other, the entrancing, if indefinite, prospects of a fuller existence that flight might have in store. It was a vision after which he flung himself; but visions, dreams, and fancies were his constant refuge from a world in which he was never at home.

Finally, the knowledge that he had been denied freedom and leisure for harmonious self-development filled him with never-ending anguish. He had become a celebrated preacher, to be sure, but the price of his eminence was crushing and the profits bitter. He had paid with his youth. Instead of living life he had taught and preached about it, probed into its past forms and speculated on its possibilities for the future. He found it no more possible than in his student-days to co-ordinate and unify the various branches of knowledge to which he turned. Yet the vision, daily more alluring, of the history of humanity filled him with an excitement that soon became intolerable. The Faust-like yearning within his soul could no longer be stilled. Every effort to keep him failed. With funds provided by friends and promising to return, Herder boarded ship on May 23, 1769, intending to go to Copenhagen to visit Klopstock and Gerstenberg, but actually proceeding to Nantes, where he arrived in July. This was the turning-point in both his life and authorship.

III. HERDER'S JOURNEY

What more was to be done except vindicate his action before his own restless eyes? For parting did not obliterate the gnawing memories of the past. In the *Journal meiner Reise*, Herder has left an analysis of his whole mental structure. In the solitude of life on board ship he looked back with horror at the grey abstractions he had left, and forward with longing to a life of action. He was well aware of his dreamy romantic nature, its impressionability and melancholy inclination towards the sublime, the sombre, and the infinite, and resolved to assess and to preserve its peculiar usefulness. That he was different from other men meant for him that he had an individual mission; his duty was to fulfil himself, in his own, and no other, way.

The journey provides the key to Herder's work. It completed the revolution in his spiritual life. What had hitherto been imperfectly thought out now leapt with novel vitality into the very forefront of his consciousness. One of a small group of primitive seamen, under iron discipline, Herder lived through the whole throbbing range of human feeling, such as he had formerly only dreamed about. Immediate experience taught him to understand its ways of operation and expression. Sailors' superstitions showed him how mythologies grew.

As he gazed at the countries he passed, he thought of the characteristics of their civilizations, and it became clearer than ever that it was his calling to study the history of the human mind in all its manifestations, at all times and in all places; to ascertain its real meaning and purpose, so as to educate, indeed regenerate, his own crumbling age. Nothing more and nothing less. Herder was primarily a teacher. It was not the contemporary fashion of universal history but his own pedagogic urge that led him to seek to understand the forces inherent in mankind, in order that he might show the future direction human effort should take in the interests of a securely founded, symmetrically developed, and harmoniously balanced system of culture.

The plans which Herder set before himself can hardly ever have been surpassed for the majesty of their conception and the turbulent profusion in which they succeed one another. He sees himself as the reformer of Livonia, and outlines a new system of schooling which shall emphasize the living realities of the immediate world. He will draft a new constitution for Russia. He will compile an anthology of the treasures of European literature; prepare a translation of the Bible and write a life of Jesus. He will study national psychologies and national cultures. He will set the sciences on a new basis. 'Universalgeschichte der Bildung der Welt'—such is his programme. It will include history, education, psychology, philosophy, language, literature, jurisprudence, natural science, theology, politics, archaeology, and the arts; every form of human self-expression, every phase of human endeavour in all nations and at all times will be treated. Language and literature, hitherto the main subjects of his writings, turn out to be but stepping-stones to the wider study of the whole of mankind.

In face of such exciting prospects France proved distinctly disappointing. Herder judged its culture to be declining, and felt himself to be growing, in contrast, more and more German in spirit. Meeting eminent thinkers, d'Alembert, d'Arnaud, Barthélemy, and others (it is doubtful if Diderot was among his acquaintances) did little to alter his impressions. An invitation negotiated by Nicolai reached him in Paris to become tutor and travelling-companion to the son of the Prince-Bishop of Lübeck, and was most acceptable, though he still clung to the hope of one day returning to Riga. He left at once for Germany, via Brussels. In January, on the voyage from Antwerp to Amsterdam, his ship grounded in the darkness. As he waited for the morning and for safety, awed by the sublimity of the elements, he read Macpherson's *Fingal*. The Ossianic feelings he read of became

c

compelling realities. The storm filled him with a sense of the nearness of the sustaining power of God:

'Hast du je, mein Freund, bei kalten dunklen Nächten, nach einer gefährlichen, grauen- und schauervollen Mitternacht . . . auf den ersten Strahl der Morgenröte gehofft, und dann den webenden Geist der Tagesfrühe gefühlt, wie er sich vor dem erwachenden Morgen, ein Hauch Gottes! ein Geist des Himmels niedersenkt und auf den Fluten wandelt! . . . Und siehe! diese Entzückung, dies unnennbare Morgengefühl, wie's scheint alle Wesen zu ergreifen! zu liegen auf der ganzen Natur! . . . wehe dem Fühllosen, der diese Szene gesehen und Gott nicht gefühlt hat!'[1]

he exclaimed in words that combine the grandiose 'sombreness' of his genius with the mystical humility of Pascal. It flashed upon him that in such an experience of the dawn by a primitive poet might lie the basis of the Creation story of the Bible. He himself now felt what it was to be a poet. With overwhelming gladness he realized that Genius was something, not merely divinely inspired, as Hamann and Young held, but emphatically a part of the divine, a prophetic medium, an interpreter of God's purpose, an agent in the never-ending work of God's Creation. This cosmic view of poetry remains a dominating element in Herder's criticism, and, in an extended application, in his philosophy.

Herder arrived at Eutin in Holstein, the Prince's capital, in March, 1770. In July he was off with his charge and passed through Hamburg, where he had stopped on his way from Holland and where he met Lessing, Claudius, and others. Italy was the ultimate destination, and by August, after visiting Hanover, Göttingen, and Kassel, the party reached Darmstadt. Here Herder met his future wife, Caroline Flachsland, who belonged to a circle of sentimentalists grouped round Merck, the friend of Goethe, and to this group Herder read and recited Klopstock's Odes. Before the end of the month the Prince's suite moved to Strassburg, and Herder, increasingly pained by his subordinate position and repeated slights, now decided to accept an invitation to become Chief Pastor to the Count of Schaumburg-Lippe. He delayed his departure, however, in order to undergo an operation to his eye in the Strassburg Faculty of Medicine, and it was not until April, 1771, that he finally arrived in Bückeburg, the Count's diminutive capital, to begin his duties.

---

[1] VI. 136 and 259; 'Have you ever, on cold dark nights, after a midnight of horror and awe, . . . hoped for the first ray of dawn, and then felt the living spirit of the day, as it comes down before the awakening of morning like a breath from God, a spirit from heaven, and moves over the waters? . . . Behold, this rapture, this nameless feeling of morning, how it seems to thrill all beings, to lie upon the whole of nature! . . . Woe to the man who has no feeling, who has seen this spectacle and has not felt God!'

The winter of 1770-1 was one of the most unhappy periods in Herder's life. The thrice performed operation did not result in a cure, and, tried to the utmost by pain and anxiety, he fretted in enforced idleness. The life of action for which he longed was again denied him. Yet in the intervals of his torment he managed to add to the *Archäologie des Morgenlandes*, which he had drafted in Riga, and to compose, in the last weeks of 1770, a prize-essay on the origin of language, a subject that had long occupied him (*Über den Ursprung der Sprache*, published in 1772).

Here, in the early autumn, began his famous friendship with Goethe, then a young law student of twenty-one. In the darkened room of Herder's inn, as he poured out his criticisms, was born the literary revolution of Germany. Here was achieved his greatest work —he showed Goethe how to be a poet. His words, harsh and over-bearing as they were, gave that living stimulus that Goethe needed at the outset of his career. He taught what Hamann had taught. He made overwhelmingly clear the poverty and artificiality of German literature. Goethe was told that originality was a universal gift, tha poetry was not the monopoly of the cultured few. He heard the Old Testament, the *Edda*, Ossian, Homer, Shakespeare, all interpreted as records of the voice of creative nature, itself the living garment of the all-pervading, all-encompassing Godhead. The message of the *Fragmente* was impressively repeated—that German poetry could only revive by emulating the originality of other literatures, that is, by basing itself upon the memorials of its own native past, the songs and legends of the people, from which alone it might derive the inspira-tion, material, and form that were congenial to it. And so, while Goethe collected Alsatian folksongs at Herder's instance, he learned to listen through them to the voice of nature from which they sprang and to see into the heart of humanity, as Herder said he would. Moreover, what Herder preached about life, Goethe learned to follow out in himself; to cultivate a full, undistorted existence, obey-ing only the inherent urge of his personality, not hindering or evading experience nor disguising self-expression, not bowing to the un-reasonable pressure of arbitrary form or convention, but seeking every means of allowing his genius full scope to fulfil its mission. Herder taught Goethe to be himself. And through Goethe he spoke to the whole of the rising generation.

IV. BÜCKEBURG

It remains to be seen how Herder's plans progressed. Two essays containing the Strassburg programme, 'Über Ossian und die Lieder alter Völker' and 'Shakespeare', which were composed shortly after his arrival in Bückeburg, were published in 1773 in the small collection *Von Deutscher Art und Kunst*. This book formed the manifesto of the national literary revival, besides advancing its author's thought materially towards its historical goal.

Herder's stay in the small Westphalian capital lasted five years and was outwardly most unhappy. Jealous colleagues and an uncongenial master drove him almost to despair. The Countess alone showed understanding—and she was a consumptive pietist who shared her melancholy yearnings with him and sought reassurance in his spiritual guidance. To be sure, Herder was now happily married to Caroline; to her unremitting encouragement the world owes the continuation of many an unfinished work, especially the more remunerative ones. To these years belongs, too, a lasting connection with Heyne, the Göttingen philologist. Herder's own protracted and unsuccessful negotiations for a chair in that University, however, only added to the anxiety caused by the suspicion and mockery with which his challenging theological writings were met.

The unrest of the journey to Nantes continued unabated. Herder was torn in all directions in his efforts to secure a good anchorage. He knew that aesthetic studies and literary criticism such as had hitherto engaged his main attention, were narrow and abstract in comparison with his ultimate task, the history of man. But how was the change from one to the other to be effected? The wish was there. How was it to be transformed into reality? Herder's imagination always ran far ahead of him, and it was his tragedy that he could not keep up with its frantic pace.

In his distress—and in the lonely desolation of his daily life—he was saved by a new religious experience. He struggled hard and long to find his place in relation to the world and to God. The Bible was always with him. He steeped himself in it as never before, and discovered new and mystical interpretations. Outwardly his behaviour was most disturbing to his suspicious flock, because it seemed as if nocturnal wanderings in the deserted countryside were his only consolation. His communings with nature stilled his yearnings, and he felt again the nearness of God, just as he had done on the night of his shipwreck.

The next stage, then, in the evolution of Herder's historical pro-gramme after its enunciation in the *Reisejournal* was that his whole outlook became unshakably fixed upon a religious basis. God's plan for mankind, from its earliest beginnings up to the Day of Judgement, this was what his many theological writings of these years sought to grasp and to expound—for he was sure, from his Biblical studies, that there was such a plan. The Bible taught him to see purpose in history —a fundamental point. Like Newman, Herder accepted religious experience as the guide and partner of research, and set revelation far above human reason as the source of knowledge. Thus did Hamann's assiduous teachings bear fruit. Logic was supplanted completely by faith.

History, then, was for Herder the story of the manifestation of God's will. He approached it with reverence and humility, as some mysterious and holy presence. To look for abstract scientific laws in it amounted in his eyes almost to sacrilege. The living forces of the world, warmth and strength and vitality, these are what he sought to apprehend and to enjoy. Theology and history became for him one and the same thing. Henceforth Herder's writings have all of them a seer-like quality about them. Beside them the literary efforts of a few years before seem tame and utilitarian.

A new, polemical, phase in Herder's authorship opened. In the strictly theological field he produced in 1774-76 the *Älteste Urkunde des Menschengeschlechts*, the outcome of his studies on Hebrew archae-ology; *An Prediger, Fünfzehn Provinzialblätter*, an historical account of the preacher's office, came in 1774—the Pascalian title was deliberately chosen; and in 1775 two essays in Biblical interpretation followed, *Erläuterungen zum Neuen Testament* and *Briefe zweener Brüder Jesu*. The other completed works of this period were the collection of English and Germanic folksongs, which was partially printed and dated 1774 but not published, the important philosophical treatise, *Auch Eine Philosophie der Geschichte zur Bildung der Menschheit* (1774), and a prize-essay, *Ursachen des gesunkenen Geschmacks* (1775). Oratorios and lyric dramas in the style of Klopstock—of which *Brutus* (1774) is the most important—belong also to these years.

Other writings remained in draft form until Herder reached Weimar. For in 1776 he accepted the Duke Karl August's offer, be-hind which stood Wieland and Goethe, of the posts of Superin-tendent, Chief Pastor, and Court Preacher. The death of the Countess Maria of Schaumburg-Lippe early in 1776, a breach with the Count, and the disturbing outcome of the Göttingen negotiations made the prospects all the more alluring.

V. WEIMAR

Herder's removal to Weimar began a less restless epoch. Many circumstances combined to withdraw him from his mystical communings and to bring him into touch with worldly things. The whole atmosphere was much more pleasing in the first place. He held high office—or rather about a dozen offices—and he was proud of his eminence and the opportunities it afforded of intervening in the cause of public education and enlightenment. His official business brought him face to face with everyday problems. He enjoyed the respect and the society of important and interesting friends—the Duchess Luise, Wieland, Knebel, Einsiedel, Prince August of Gotha, and Frau von Schardt; and above all there was Goethe, still an ardent admirer and now the all-powerful adviser of the Duke. Yet, through Herder's jealousy, a breach soon came about. He was no more destined to find lasting happiness in Weimar than in Bückeburg. Unceasing dissatisfaction, Faust-like yearnings, obstinacy and excessive sensitivity, all reacted to his detriment. His censoriousness alienated many, and even his friendship with Hamann was at one time endangered.

Nevertheless, conditions remained agreeable sufficiently long for the change in Herder's outlook to be completed. The religious view of history, though retaining its essentials, grew less unworldly. He read widely in philosophy and natural science. His vision expanded, its lopsidedness in the religious direction was corrected and it was soon ripe enough to be set out in detail. This is the contribution of the Weimar years. The change is evident, too, in his style, which is clearer and calmer than ever before. The violent prejudices and extreme intolerance of the Bückeburg years recede, and we are reminded more and more of the seraphic side of Herder that Anton Graff recorded in his portrait. Never since the earliest Riga days had there been anything to suggest this quality.

The first few years were extremely fruitful. On the theological side came the *Lieder der Liebe* (1778), a translation of the 'Song of Solomon' with an appreciation of it as Hebrew love-poetry, and the highly mystical *Maran Atha, das Buch von der Zukunft des Herrn* (1779). The *Briefe, das Studium der Theologie betreffend* (1780-1) demanded a more liberal outlook in theological training, while *Vom Geiste der Ebräischen Poesie* (1782-3) is the most famous of all his interpretations of the Bible. From Bückeburg, Herder also brought two works on psychology, *Vom Erkennen und Empfinden* (1778), which studies the interaction of feeling and thought, and the *Plastik* (1778), an account of the process of artistic production. The 1774 collection of folksongs grew into the *Volkslieder* of 1778-9, the work by which Herder is now most widely remembered. Three further prize-essays, concerned largely with defining the educational function of poetry—*Über die Wirkung der Dichtkunst* (1778), *Über den Einfluß der schönen in die höheren Wissenschaften* (1779), and *Vom Einfluß der Regierungen auf die Wissenschaften und der Wissenschaften auf die Regierung* (1780)—complete the harvest of these years.

The decade 1783-93 saw a renewal of Herder's friendship with Goethe. The latter was well aware of the difficulties with which his friend wrestled and of their origin in his unharmonious nature, and did his best to help Herder to overcome them. The two regularly exchanged views on scientific topics. Both were convinced of the inherent unity of nature, the simplicity of her beginnings, and the rising complexity of her creations; both were concerned with human existence and the scene of its activity. It is to these years of happy and sympathetic collaboration that the peak of Herder's achievement belongs, the realization of his plan of a history of mankind in his *Ideen zur Philosophie der Geschichte der Menschheit* (1784-91), the work for which all his previous efforts had been in the nature of preparation. Goethe was in close touch with the genesis of this book and he exercised a salutary effect as the composition proceeded, by supporting his friend's speculations with the tangible results of his own scientific investigations. For Herder's conclusions too often rested upon poetic intuitions and ingenious fancies.

The *Ideen*, characteristically, remained unfinished. A final section was planned, but never executed. Much of the unused material passed into other works. The religious background was developed in the *Gott* of 1787 and in the *Christliche Schriften* of 1794-98, the apex of his theological work, containing some of the most beautiful of all his writings. A large collection of essays and poems, *Zerstreute Blätter* (1785-97), illustrates the same moral preoccupations and the same desire to understand the teachings of history as the *Ideen*. A renovation, in German verse, of the Latin work of the seventeenth-century Jesuit poet, Jacob Balde, the *Terpsichore* (1795-6), had some important repercussions.

The events of the French Revolution turned Herder's attention to practical problems and led him to formulate his political views afresh. The patriotism which he proclaimed demanded that all the native powers of the people should be developed, not only for the sake of national unity and strength but also in the interest of civilization as a whole. With undaunted enthusiasm, he strove hard to convince Germany of her latent possibilities, to present her with the most elevated ideals, and to teach her to take her place as an equal among other nations, in order that the harmony of human culture might be completed. This was the chief purpose of the *Briefe zu Beförderung der Humanität* (1793-97) and of Herder's last work, the *Adrastea* (1801-04). The latter contains one of his most famous productions, a German version of the story of the Cid.

Enduring happiness was never Herder's lot. His irritability and ineradicable dissatisfaction were increased by the indifference of the outside world to his teaching. Difficulties met him on every side in his self-appointed task of supervising and revitalizing Weimar culture. As it was, did not most people deny its necessity? However, some achievements were of immediate practical significance. In the matter of school reform he succeeded in improving both method and curriculum, and his zeal for raising the status and the pay of teachers led to the foundation of a training college in 1788. His efforts in the Church to obtain more sincerity in the services took the form of a new liturgy and a series of cantata texts, including the German libretto of Handel's *Messiah*. To be sure, that was scant satisfaction, in face of his far-reaching intentions.

Weimar was not the place for a man of his temperament. He knew it, and was never free from regrets after he refused a call to a Göttingen professorship in 1788. A disappointing Italian journey in 1788-9 marks the beginning of a steady decline. Recurring illness, constant financial difficulties, the irksomeness of official duties, the estrangement from Goethe and Schiller, and, above all, the oppressive sense of failure that never left him, all contributed to his unhappiness. In spite of this, he was as full of new plans as ever. The more interesting include translations of the Bible, of Pindar, Horace, Ossian (from the 'original' Gaelic), and of some of Shakespeare's plays, a history of poetry and a survey of Greek mythology. But the disproportion between purpose and achievement weighed as heavily as it did in the Riga years. Only now he was no longer young. In fancy he constructed a little ideal world of his own, peopled only by his immediate circle. In his gloom he gave way more and more to melancholy forebodings, read deeply in the literature of Mysticism, and paid serious attention to dreams and omens. The tragedy of his life was completed by the bitterness of his unsuccessful campaign against his former teacher Kant, waged in the *Metakritik zur Kritik der reinen Vernunft* (1799) and *Kalligone* (1800). Finally, his acceptance in 1802 of a patent of Bavarian nobility was a tactless affront that alienated the Court circle almost completely from him.

He died, an utterly disappointed man, on the 18th December, 1803. The life of action for which he sighed had eluded him to the end. From the prosaic imperfections of actuality he had sought refuge in the world of dreams and ideals. This was the world that claimed him. It turned out to be a prison from which there was no escape.

CHAPTER III

THE APPROACH TO LITERATURE

JEAN Paul Richter, a devoted admirer, once said of Herder that he was not a star of the first magnitude but a collection of stars. He shone in many fields of thought; and though his radiance was often thickened and diffused, it pierced into recesses whose existence was previously unsuspected. To others was left the task of completer exploration, while Herder, with gnarling sorrow, was fated to watch them draw—as men still draw to this day—the profits of his discoveries. His mantle fell, not on any one man in particular, but upon a whole nation and an entire generation. This, as Goethe pointed out, was the reason for his being forgotten and unread. For each individual, from Herder's own day, has been conscious only of that particular fold that touched him and unaware of the real size and cut of the mantle, as well as of its original ownership. So Herder's memorial consists of the strivings and achievements of the many who came after him. It was to the future that he always looked; but can he ever have imagined how deeply his message would ultimately resound or how far its echo would carry?

The character of Herder's authorship is suggested by the title of his first major work, the *Fragmente*. Of his numerous writings none, excepting his poems, is complete in itself. All supplement something that has gone before or prepare the way for something that is to come. None exhausts a subject but rather floods it with comment and suggestion. Herder's mind refused to submit to the ordinary requirements of form. No form could cope with its constantly expanding material. He culled from many and varied sources, his thoughts flowed so inexhaustibly that he was quite unable to fuse them into one coherent and satisfying system and concentrate upon each point in its turn and in its place, else some valuable part of his commentary would inevitably be lost in the process. He was swept into speaking his thoughts to the world, as soon as they crossed his mind, by that dominating passion of his existence, the urge to teach. From the start he was haunted by a crushing sense of impending doom; the lightning, which he knew in his bones would rive modern culture to the sand on which it was built, flickered even as he toiled at the way to safety. But he toiled in isolation, and therefore the more furiously, all the time uttering fevered exhortations, mingled with censure, to silent, uninterested bystanders. It was a desperate race, with all the odds against him; but as long as life lasted he never gave up.

It is not surprising that there is something haphazard about Herder's writings, as if his thoughts had been flung on to paper. It always seems as if he elaborates what he has to say, *after*, not *before*, publication—i.e. in other works. His programme pieced itself together as he grew older and learned more. Inevitably there are faulty joints, gaps, repetitions, clashes, and contradictions. He was forever rearranging and supplementing, and whenever he came to revise an earlier work or draft, nothing less than a complete re-casting of the whole plan was the invariable result. The seeds of his later achievement are thus to be found in his first works. It is misleading, however, for readers merely to attend to the early writings. Only from what amplifies them can a complete picture be drawn. It is as one-sided to read the *Fragmente* without the *Humanitätsbriefe* as to read the *Humanitätsbriefe* without the *Fragmente*. Still, it is surprising how often this is done, and how often critics have been reduced to helplessness or unintelligent repetition of one another.

No major writer was hampered by so unsatisfying a style as Herder. He never wrote with precision. He was repetitive, admonitory, ejaculatory. He indulged in picturesque, telling, even extravagant metaphors, but was lacking in adroitness. His drafts and sketches show him constantly and painfully struggling for the means of adequate utterance. He knew what he wanted to say and that it needed to be said. Yet he could not achieve a balanced and coherent form in which to say it. Even his syntax breaks down at times. In the excitement of his earlier works, anger, bitterness, sarcasm, reproach, exhortation are communicated in the abruptest and most confusing manner. His language, nevertheless, never fails to be effective, by reason of its very energy. Herder was a man in whom feeling and imagination ran ahead of expression. He was at his best when delivering his message orally, from the pulpit or in conversation. Writing was too much of a fetter for his all-too-fertile mind. It is only in his later works that anything approaching harmony and smoothness can be discerned, and the *Ideen* and kindred writings contain passages of great poetic beauty.

When he began to write, Herder regarded Germany, with justice, as culturally a subject nation, stupified by the imitation of foreign— Classical and French—models; and imperfectly understood models at that. The further he got with his work, the clearer this thought grew, and the more pressing was the need for a remedy. The *Fragmente* began in a small way from the idea of composing a running commentary on Lessing's *Litteraturbriefe.* Though Herder largely concurred in Lessing's findings, it was quickly obvious that two fundamentally different methods were face to face, and that the older critic was left well behind. If Herder supported his predecessor's attacks on the followers of Gottsched and Bodmer and his complaints against the lack of originality in modern German literature, he could not share his unquestioning attachment to the example of the Ancients. In Herder's eyes all writers were equally justified. It was not for him to say whether a poet stood or fell by the achievements of the Ancients, but rather to ascertain what purpose he had in mind and whether he fulfilled it or not—not whether he fulfilled some other purpose. He sought to understand rather than to judge; not to measure with dogmatic authority but to discover why a work was as it was. His method was founded on the principle of historical investigation. He studied origins and developments, environmental causes and peculiarities of creative genius. Unusual gifts of divination and assimilation helped him to trace emotions and ideas back to their sources in an author's mind, to transfer himself into the circumstances of time and place in which he worked, re-think his thoughts, re-feel his feelings, share his hopes and endeavours. Herder's approach was sympathetic and appreciative. Before all else he respected the sanctity of individuality—and individuality included everything that contributes to its formation.

'Es bleibt auch die unentbehrlichste Erklärung insonderheit eines Dichters, die Erklärung seiner Zeit- und Nationalsitten.'[1]

'So lange man nicht Ideen in ihre Quelle zurückzulenken weiß, in den Sinn des Schriftstellers, so schreibt man höchstens wider ihn, und erregt . . . statt Überzeugung Widerspruch.'[2]

'Dem Schriftsteller, was soll der Kunstrichter sein? Sein Diener, sein Freund, sein unparteiischer Richter! Suche ihn kennen zu lernen und als deinen Herrn auszustudieren, nicht aber dein eigner Herr sein zu wollen. . . . Es ist schwer, aber billig, daß der Kunstrichter sich in den Gedankenkreis seines Schriftstellers versetze und aus seinem Geist lese.'[3]

---

[1] II. 161; 'The most indispensable explanation of a poet especially is the explanation of the customs of his age and nation.'

[2] I. 142; 'If we do not trace ideas back to their source, back to the author's mind, at the most we write against him and produce disagreement instead of conviction.'

[3] I. 247; 'What is the critic to be to the author? His servant, his friend, his impartial judge. Seek to get to know him and to make a thorough study of him as your master, but seek not to be your own master. . . . It is difficult, but just, that the critic should transfer himself into the thoughts of his author and read him in the spirit in which he wrote.'

Complete self-surrender to the work under examination, that was Herder's objective. Only a short step divides such criticism from history, as he well knew.

It is difficult to realize how much this method meant to a generation of authors, who were looked upon and who looked upon themselves as prisoners standing their trial before a court administering the laws of the Greeks and the Romans. When Herder showed that these laws did not possess universal validity but applied only to the Greeks and Romans, it took the Germans by surprise. They needed to accustom themselves to their unexpected freedom; they dared hardly avail themselves of it until Goethe boldly gave them a lead.

The result was as Herder had intended. He held it to be his duty, and that of criticism, to promote national culture. Criticism could discharge this duty best by proceeding as he did—a natural enough conclusion! It should interpret rather than arraign, it should show the way in which excellence was attained by past or present writers, so that others might follow it for themselves.

The kinship of Herder's sympathetic attitude with that evolved by Sainte-Beuve and later criticism is obvious. His work indeed represented a turning-point. He gathered together the most valuable achievements of the past and made them fruitful—more fruitful than he knew—for the future. As has already been mentioned, his debt to predecessors was great—which was inevitable in one so widely read. It would be futile to attempt to assess it in detail, but certain obvious names stand out. The Scottish critic Blackwell, in a book which Herder highly esteemed, *Enquiry into the Life and Writings of Homer* (1735), investigated Homer's debt to his *milieu* and discovered the common origin of poetry and language in song, thereby anticipating much in both the matter and method of the *Fragmente*. Winckelmann's history of Greek art (1764) directly inspired Herder with the demand for, and the desire to be, a Winckelmann of Greek literature, and it was no great step further to apply Winckelmann's point of view to literature in general and to German literature in particular. Finally Herder's own teachers, Kant and Hamann, left their unmistakable mark. The former taught him to probe for basic principles; the latter reinforced this by urging him to look to the very beginnings of things if he were to understand them, and to rely upon the guidance of feeling rather than reason, in appreciating the importance of any author's work.

The themes discussed in the *Fragmente* had occupied Herder since his student days. Among his first plans had been one of a history of the ode. Encouraged by Hamann, he was fascinated by the twin problems of the origin of poetry in general and of the lyric in particular. That poetry was the mother-tongue of the human race and that the earliest form of poetry was song are constantly recurring ideas. Herder saw, as well, that literature had a cultural function, and in a short essay, 'Über den Fleiß in mehreren gelehrten Sprachen' (1764), had already raised his voice in favour of literary patriotism, calling for a more balanced attitude in regard to the imitation of other countries, so that the national stock and national originality should be strengthened and not impaired as had been hitherto the case.

These were the more immediate topics that busied Herder. His copious notes and sketches alone convey an idea of the pertinacity, penetration, and earnestness with which he worked. In these early years he not only prepared himself for the *Fragmente*, but conceived the programme of his whole life's work, so that there is scarcely a point of major importance that is not foreshadowed in some way. According to Herder's original plan, there were to have been four sections, dealing in turn with language, aesthetics, history, and philosophy. But, as he wrote, two themes became uppermost in his mind—the relationship between language and literature, and the relationship between German literature and its models.

Under the first heading, Herder tried to discover the genius of German language, so as to determine and even forecast the kind of poetry it would be capable of producing and thus reveal its latent possibilities to intending authors. 'Der Genius der Sprache', he writes, 'ist also auch der Genius von der Literatur einer Nation.'[1] Developing the results of Blackwell, Winckelmann, and Hamann, with perhaps a hint or two from Hugh Blair's *Critical Dissertation on the Poems of Ossian* (1763), of which he had seen extracts, he distinguished, after the analogy of human life, four ages of language; firstly, the childhood of language, the age of inarticulate beginnings governed entirely by stress of feeling; secondly, youth, when linguistic symbols become more ordered and rhythmical and the first signs of abstract thought appear in the form of imagery and metaphor, with the emotional basis still remaining in its pristine strength—and this, according to Herder, is the age of poetry; thirdly, manhood, the age of prose, poetry having ceased to be the direct expression of nature and become art, and language being remarkable less for its directness and vigour than for its orderly arrangement and seriousness; and finally, old age, the period of philosophy, when correctness of expression out-

---

[1] I. 148; 'The genius of a nation's language is thus also the genius of its literature.'

weighs every other consideration. It was this analogy with human life that appealed to Hegel. Herder's opinion was that German had reached the age of prose, but argued that in the future both 'serious prose and profound poetry' were possible. German had aged prematurely and unnaturally, having been denied, as he knew *he* had been, the joy and freshness of youth. He was convinced that the destiny of the German language was unfulfilled, that it was still in the process of formation. Its native strength was still untapped. He analysed its speech-sounds on phonetic lines, he pointed to its syntactical characteristics, its strength of idiom, its 'inversions,' its *Machtworte* and *Klangworte*.

'Unsere Sprache ist reich an Idiotismen, und Idiotismen sind patronymische Schönheiten und gleichen jenen heiligen Ölbäumen, die rings um die Akademie bei Athen ihrer Schutzgöttin Minerva geweiht waren. Ihre Frucht durfte nicht aus Attika gehen und war bloß der Lohn der Sieger am panathenäischen Feste. Ja, da die Lazedämonier einst alles verwüsteten, so ließ die Göttin es nicht zu, daß diese fremden Barbaren ihre Hände an diesen heiligen Hain legten. Ebenso sind die Idiotismen Schönheiten, die uns kein Nachbar durch eine Übersetzung entwenden kann, und die der Schutzgöttin der Sprache heilig sind; Schönheiten, in das Genie der Sprache verwebt, die man zerstört, wenn man sie austrennet; Reize, die durch die Sprache, wie der Busen der Phryne durch einen seidenen Nebel, durch das Wassergewand der alten Statuen, das sich an die Haut anschmiegt, durchschimmern.'[1]

Herder felt therefore—and here his analogy is not quite consistent—that while possessing the ability to go forward to the age of philosophy, German could, if encouraged and guided, recapture the latent emotional and poetic content it had so far had no chance of exploiting owing to Latin and French domination, and thus become a powerful vehicle of poetic expression. That this second course was more than a vague probability was made clear to Herder by Klopstock's creative achievement. Herder realized better than most men how much the rich natural beauty of his mother-tongue had been overshadowed, and how great the loss had been that German litera-

---

[1] II. 44; 'Our language is rich in idioms, and idioms are patronymic beauties and are like those sacred olive-trees around the Athenian Academy which were dedicated to its protecting goddess Minerva. Their fruits could not leave Attica and served only as rewards to the victors in the Panathenian festival. Indeed, when the Spartans once laid all things waste, the goddess did not permit the barbarians to lay their hands upon this sacred grove. In this manner, idioms are beauties that no neighbour can take from us in translation, and which are sacred to the protecting goddess of language; beauties woven into the genius of language, which are destroyed if they are taken out of it; charms which show through language, as the bosom of Phryne through a silken veil, or through the transparent, clinging drapery of ancient statues.'

ture had suffered in consequence. He began that movement that has
continued until our own day in Germany, the industrious, even
feverish, endeavour, based upon poetic intuition to a greater extent
than upon reason, to regain lost ground; the rankling grudge against
fate for having been cheated of her due, in all spheres; the powerful
effort to acquire for herself what other countries have possessed for so
long; the claim for equality and a place in the sun. Herder started
this in the field of language and literature.

He was not so narrow as to deny that German could not learn from
other languages, but never again must it submit to outside influence
so far as to surrender its identity and independence. These should
rather be preserved and enlarged by usage.

'Nicht um meine Sprache zu verlernen', he says, 'lerne ich andre
Sprachen, nicht um die Sitten meiner Erziehung umzutauschen, reise ich unter
fremde Völker; nicht um das Bürgerrecht meines Vaterlandes zu verlieren,
werde ich ein naturalisierter Fremder: denn sonst verliere ich mehr, als
ich gewinne. Sondern ich gehe bloß durch fremde Gärten, um für meine
Sprache, als eine Verlobte meiner Denkart, Blumen zu holen: ich sehe
fremde Sitten, um die meinigen, wie Früchte, die eine fremde Sonne
gereift hat, dem Genius meines Vaterlandes zu opfern.'[1]

This declaration recalls forcibly what he had said in his earliest piece
of criticism in 1764:

'Unsre Schritte in fremden Gegenden werden kürzer und gewisser, wenn
das Ziel unseres Vaterlandes uns stets in die Augen blickt ... Wenn wir
unsre Muttersprache auf der Zunge behalten, so werden wir desto
tiefer in den Unterschied jeder Sprache eindringen. Hier werden wir
Lücken, dort Überfluß, hier Reichtum, dort eine Wüste erblicken; und die
Armut der einen mit den Schätzen der andern bereichern können.'[2]

Herder's second major theme is partly contained in the first.
Having made Germans conscious of the poetic possibilities of their
language, he turned to a kindred sphere and proclaimed the idea of
literary nationalism. He looked upon language and poetry as growths
organically determined by environment, by cultural, geographical,

---

[1] I. 401; 'I do not learn other languages in order to forget my own; I do not travel among
foreign peoples, in order to exchange the customs of my upbringing; I do not become an
acclimatized foreigner in order to lose the citizenship of my native-land; for if I do I lose
more than I gain. But I walk through other gardens merely to gather flowers for my mother-
tongue, the betrothed of my thought; I look upon other customs, in order to offer up mine,
like fruits ripened by a foreign sun, to the genius of my native land.'

[2] I. 6; 'Our journeys in foreign parts will be shorter and our steps surer, if the goal of our
native-land is constantly facing us. ... If we keep our native language upon our tongues, we
shall pierce more deeply into the different characters of each language. Here we shall see
deficiencies, there superfluity, here wealth, there a desert; and we shall be able to enrich the
poverty of the one with the treasures of the other.'

and political conditions. This far-reaching conception—which Herder was the first to evolve in Germany—incalculably altered the whole outlook in criticism. Poetry at once ceased to be the monopoly of the Ancients, whom it was the Moderns' duty to imitate. The Classics were dislodged from their position of absolute authority and placed in one of relative importance. Good poetry might exist equally well, if differently, away from Greece and Rome. It springs from feelings that are common to all men. It is the mother-tongue of mankind. From this, it follows that no two literatures can be alike, because of the different surroundings in which they grow up. Any attempts to model one upon another are therefore not only unnatural but definitely pernicious, since they interfere with free individual development. The extended application of this discovery of Herder's to other fields needs no emphasis at this stage. The theme recurs from the beginning to the end of his writings. The course for German literature, then, was obvious. It must henceforth seek salvation in its own way, from its own sources, just as others—the Greeks themselves —had done, by drawing upon itself alone and its own past. Just as Greek poetry grew from native foundations and reached a high degree of excellence without outside help, so German poetry should and could do the same, finding out its inherent strength and its direction and cultivating this without regard to what others did.

It was a shrewd thrust of Herder's to clinch this argument with the example of the Classics; it cut off the enemy's retreat completely and rendered any further engagement on the same ground impossible. The teachings of Hamann and Young, which may be conveniently summarized in the two Classical injunctions proclaimed in the latter's *Conjectures on Original Composition*: 'Know thyself' and 'Reverence thyself', thus acquired under Herder's hand a national significance. As none had done before and many have done since, he exhorted Germany to know itself and reverence itself; to ignore the inroads made by foreign influences, to go back to the unspoilt native sources of the Middle Ages and the sixteenth century, in which, thanks to Bodmer's pioneer work, interest was then being aroused; to seek out, as other nations had done and were doing, its own poetic treasures, its own *Nationallieder*, and follow their inspiration, since they alone were genuine and characteristic. Herder became more and more convinced as time went on that the Renaissance, and what followed it, had made an immense breach in German literature and culture, and that some means of bridging the gap, of rejoining the present with the achievements of the Middle Ages, must be found, if progress were

D

to be made. This was a task that he himself strove hard to carry out; and his message, accurate or not in its data, was the most potent and suggestive that German criticism had yet heard.

All this did not mean that Herder was prepared to look with disdain on the examples of other countries; he was as sure as any man could be that much could be learnt from them. It merely meant that imitation should give way to appreciation—a very reasonable and significant requirement. The study of others could reveal much about the real nature of poetry and its production, and native writers, if they were armed with such information, would be better able to discharge their duty. Was it not an intelligent reading of other countries' examples that had led Herder himself to his conclusions? It was natural, therefore, that he should emphasize Lessing's demand for good translations. A translator, he saw, could reveal and reproduce the sources and processes of poetic creation in other nations. His work in this respect would resemble that of the critic. If successful, he could be the 'morning-star' of a new epoch in German literature. 'Der Übersetzer muß selbst ein schöpferisches Genie sein';[1] his work would be 'eine Originalarbeit, die mehr Einfluß auf unsere Literatur haben kann als zehn Originalwerke'.[2] It would emerge as the result of sympathetic penetration into the spirit and *milieu* of the original, and would bring out the beauties and genius of a foreign literature so forcibly as to be a constant source of instruction, more valuable than any number of philological notes and explanations.

The *Kritische Wälder* approached the themes of the *Fragmente* from another angle. Once more Herder's starting-point was the work of Lessing, this time the *Laokoon*, which had drawn the dividing line between poetry and painting. The historical approach soon led Herder to reject Lessing's hasty generalizations, which had been derived, as he observed, from the doubtful example of Homer alone. His own contentions had the support of a new Homer—Ossian. For instance, Lessing had declared that the ability to combine heroism with tears was a characteristic of the cultured Greeks as opposed to the uncultured Trojans. The younger critic pronounces it to be typical, not of one nation, but of a whole phase in human culture, the border-line between nature and refinement. The spurious example of Ossian sanctioned that growing sentimentality which was soon to flood German literature, and to reach its peak in *Werther*. On such

---

[1] I. 178; 'The translator must himself be a creative genius.'
[2] I. 274; 'An original achievement of more influence upon German literature than ten original works.'

uncertain evidence was founded one of the most influential literary forces.

Herder was assailing the narrow view that exalted the Greeks as models. He considered them, just as he considered other nations, in their historical perspective—no more. In this he took his place in the rising movement that was soon to bring about the most remarkable achievements in Classical scholarship. The immediate consequence was, however, the emergence of a new attitude to Homer. Whereas Lessing and others had looked on him as a conscious artist, striving after definite effects, Herder saw him as a creative, natural poet working according to the impulse of his genius, whose greatness was determined largely by the propitious times to which he belonged. He would hear nothing, therefore, of those poetic artifices which Lessing had attributed to Homer, such as that of deliberately 'translating' description into movement, so as to fit in with the peculiar requirement that poetry should represent bodily objects indirectly through action. Indeed, he disposed of the point altogether by objecting that it was anyway the nature of the epic to narrate rather than to describe.

Herder demurred to Lessing's distinction between painting, as representing objects co-existing in space—or bodies—, and poetry, as representing objects consecutive in time—or actions. He declared that whereas the painter works with colours, which are natural symbols, the poet uses the ordinary sounds of language, which are arbitrary and therefore do not stand in the same relationship to what they represent as colours do. Lessing's distinction was thus seen to be ill-founded, because his comparisons were inaccurate. Herder differentiated more finely. He was concerned not with how poets *should* work and what effects they *should* aim at, but with how they *have* worked and *do* work; with the source of their creativeness, rather than the means which they employ. In face of Lessing's drastic pronouncement that action and not description is the real business of poetry, hardly a writer would stand guiltless, he declared. For Herder saw poetry to be the self-expression of the soul through words, and this is the root of its peculiar effectiveness, or 'energy', to use the term which he had adopted from the English philosopher Harris. This consists in the power the poet exercises over the souls of his hearers, the progressive effect of feeling on feeling, an effect that is achieved, not *after*, as Lessing had said, but *during* the process of poetic declamation.

'Wenn ich eins von Homer lerne, so ists's, daß Poesie energisch wirke; nie in der Absicht, um bei dem letzten Zuge ein Werk, Bild, Gemälde (obwohl sukzessive) zu liefern, sondern daß schon während der Energie die ganze Kraft empfunden und gefühlt werden müsse. Ich lerne von Homer, daß die Wirkung der Poesie nie aufs Ohr, durch Töne, nicht aufs Gedächtnis, wie lange ich einen Zug aus der Sukzession behalte, sondern auf meine Phantasie wirke; von hieraus also, sonst nirgendsher, berechnet werden müsse. So stelle ich sie gegen die Malerei und beklage, daß Hr. L(essing) diesen Mittelpunkt des Wesens der Poesie, "Wirkung auf unsre Seele, Energie," nicht zum Augenmerke genommen.'[1]

In other words, Herder shifted the emphasis from the intellect to the emotions, from conscious art to unconscious impulse. The spontaneous, lyrical element was now firmly established by criticism as the essential thing in poetry. The poet's natural duty was seen to be to cultivate and communicate passion. There was no further case to be made out for Classical dogma. All was ready for the overflowing emotionalism of the coming generation of *Stürmer und Dränger*.

The fourth *Wäldchen*, which remained unpublished, brought criticism into close contact with psychology. It sketched a system of aesthetics which paid attention to all the creative powers of the soul. The time-honoured arbitrary standards in literature gave way to a study of individual circumstances and *milieu*, to an analysis of psychic factors, fancy, judgement, memory, the particular state of development of the senses and emotions, and the proportions in which these are combined with one another. This is more than literary criticism. Herder looked two ways. He set out to rejuvenate German literature, as always; but he was also aware of a wider issue. Those inherent sources of originality spoken of in the *Fragmente* were now to be uncovered, in this *Wäldchen* and in later works. This was clearly something that brought him closely into touch with the study of mankind as a whole. From being a critic he was becoming an historian of humanity. The intentions of the *Fragmente* were working themselves out. The plan of the *Reisejournal* was already in being.

A kindred field shows this same transition of thought—the origin of language. Here Herder was faced with the current theories of the divine origin of language on the one hand, and its human invention at

[1] III. 157; 'If I learn one thing from Homer it is that poetry produces its effect through energy; its effect never comes from the intention of creating, down to the last detail, a work, a picture, or a description (even though there is a succession of details), but from the intention that its whole power should be experienced and realized actually during the output of energy in its presentation. I learn from Homer that the effect of poetry is never that of sound upon the ear; nor is it upon the memory, however long I can retain any particular detail out of the whole succession of details, but upon the fancy; and it must be evaluated from this standpoint, and from none other. It is from this angle that I oppose it to painting, and regret that Mr. Lessing has not had in mind this central factor in the nature of poetry, this "emotional effect, or energy".'

the hands of some kind of scholar on the other. He rejected both, since they presupposed man's possession of the capacity to receive or learn language—the power of reason. Instead, he took into account the gradual evolution of speech from elemental emotional expressions. Thus he approached the modern standpoint; but he did not agree that the inarticulate sounds which are common both to man and to the higher animals constitute language. Language was for him a human possession only, since its existence would be impossible but for the power of reflection (*Besonnenheit* Herder called it, nicely discriminating between it and reason), which is a specifically human gift and which has developed along with language. The close association of the growth of speech with that of thought and culture was stressed as a matter of course. Herder brought out the historical importance of primitive literatures as keys to the understanding of the phases to which they belonged, and ultimately to the understanding of the human mind generally. It was clearer than ever to him that poetry was a universal possession, since its origin, with that of speech, in impulse and feeling, was common to mankind. And when Herder expatiated on the forcefulness and boldness, the irregularity and figurativeness of primitive literature, it is impossible not to be aware of his dual outlook—the historian's, rejoicing in data about the past, and the critic's, eager to point out, as he had done in the *Fragmente*, the way to a revival in the future. The essay *Über den Ursprung der Sprache* stands on the border-line between the old and the new in Herder's criticism.

Here is a major step forward in Herder's lifelong task of studying the history of man. He moves nearer to the main themes contained in his central work. Fundamental to all his effort is the observation of humanity through its self-expression in language and literature. Language is in his eyes 'a dictionary of the soul', a mirror of culture. It derives from the special place of man in the cosmos and reflects his relationship to it. As the vehicle of thought, language transmits all knowledge and experience. Speech and intellect develop hand in hand. Language is both the offspring and the guide of thought. Man is, therefore, not only the creator of language but its creature as well. He reveals himself in it, and it determines his self-revelation. It expresses all the workings of his soul, and his soul is an indivisible unity of manifold powers and impulses. Language, thus, is the key to the whole understanding of man and his position within the universe.

The psychology of the human mind is involved in Herder's programme. The origins and operations of knowledge and the emotions must at once come under his scrutiny. The poet, as a creator of language, and his place in human society present another topic. Further, since man emerges as a social being, as a member of a group, the nation, in which language maintains itself historically, reveals itself as being of prime importance. In fine, the study of language leads to the study of all the human race in its manifold self-revelations in all places and at all times. The way to history was becoming ever clearer.

Behind all this, despite Herder's rejection of the theory of the supernatural origin of language in which Hamann believed, stood the latter's novel teaching, that language is God made manifest in the Word; the Word communicated ever anew, on the one hand in nature and man's efforts to understand her throughout history, and on the other in the commentary to all things provided by the Bible. No greater and more instructive task awaited Herder than that set him by language, its origin and development. All his subsequent thought is fundamentally affected by it. His history takes language— and literature—as its most revealing source of information. Never perhaps at any time has language been viewed in its widest context so fruitfully as by Herder. It need hardly be said that all later philosophy of language has drawn inspiration from his work.

CHAPTER IV

FOLK-POETRY

HERDER'S Bückeburg works show a turbulence that reflects the far-reaching change that his thought was undergoing. He was in search of a new centre of gravity. The process of finding it was long and difficult. The sea-journey was just the beginning. It gave only the plan. The execution was still to come. Yet all the while Herder had so much to say and could not keep it back, like a prophet all too conscious of the need to deliver his message, even though it was not yet under control. Hence the excitement, abruptness, and pugnacity of his writings of the Bückeburg years. The essays on Ossian and Shakespeare, the first of this numerous series, show all the signs of his agitation. His thoughts are tumbled out in overwhelming profusion, without any regard for formal effect. The ordinary reader finds it hard to keep up with their torrential sweep. In these breathless pages full-stops and commas seem like unnatural intruders. There were special reasons, however, in this case for Herder's electrifying exuberance. His reading of Ossian and Shakespeare precipitated one of the most influential movements in modern literature, the cult of folk-poetry, *Volkslied*, *Volkspoesie*.

James Macpherson's Ossianic poems had made their first appearance in three volumes—*Fragments of Ancient Poetry* (1760), *Fingal* (1762), and *Temora* (1763). Including the *Fragments*, nearly all of which were absorbed into the longer poems, there were two epics and twenty shorter pieces, all purporting to be translations from the Gaelic original of the Celtic bard Ossian, the son of Fingal, who lived in the third century. Dr. Hugh Blair's famous *Critical Dissertation on the Poems of Ossian* appeared in 1763. The moment was as propitious for Ossian's appearance in German form as in English. The publication of Middle High German poetry by Bodmer; Klopstock's glorification of the Germanic past, in which he confused Celts and Germans and Norsemen; the printing of specimens of the *Edda* in the supplement to Mallet's widely circulated *Introduction à l'histoire de Dannemarc* (1765-6), with the consequent expansion of Norse studies; and finally the beginnings of patriotic feeling in German literature, springing largely, but not exclusively, from the glamorous excitement of Frederick the Great's campaigns—these circumstances alone made the atmosphere eminently suitable. But there were other factors. The popularity of the poetry of melancholy reflection and the grave, the delight in tender sentimentality and moralizing lachrymosity, the admiration for the nature descriptions of such men as Kleist and Gessner, the growing attention to the poetry and supposed ideal humanity of primitive races—these interests were also satisfied by the new poet. German literature was already making headway towards the light of day, when a shaft of phantom radiance from the bard, at once helpful and somewhat dazzling, drew it headlong forward. The wild grandeur of his grey and misty landscapes formed an impressive background for the bravery and blameless nobility of his heroes. The supernatural was present in a form suggestive of a new national mythology. The narratives were full of simplicity and pathos, while their rhythmic prose style, modelled on that of the Old Testament and containing many Homeric and Miltonic touches, could not fail to attract. Ossian possessed so many qualities that appealed to the eighteenth century; and to these the authority of his presumed genuineness gave the hall-mark of naturalness and antiquity. At the same time he was sufficiently strange to excite general curiosity.

Specimens began to appear in Germany as early as 1762, but the principal translations were Engelbrecht's *Fragmente* and Wittenberg's *Fingal*, both published in Hamburg in 1764, and both, like the English original, in prose. The hexameter version by Denis, of which the first two volumes were issued in 1768 and the third in 1769, was the first complete German translation, and included, besides Macpherson's introductions and notes, Blair's *Dissertation*, of which only extracts had been translated before. Previously only *Fingal* and ten of the shorter poems—decidedly the better part of the whole—were known in German garb, and it was therefore easy for an exaggerated opinion of Ossian's excellence to arise which would be difficult to extinguish, especially if allowance were made for the quality of the German version, as being itself the translation of a 'translation'. Doubts regarding the authenticity were not taken seriously except by Gerstenberg in his *Briefe über die Merkwürdigkeiten der Litteratur*.

Herder was quickly attracted. Hamann had prepared the way, but he almost certainly did not introduce him to the bard, for Hamann mentions Ossian very seldom, and it was not until 1769 that he ordered a copy for himself. In the meantime—probably in 1765— Herder, whose interest in popular poetry was already evident, had acted for himself. The revelation was gradual and, for long, incomplete. As he himself informs us, he was abreast of the main German publications—that is all. Up to the time of leaving Riga he knew the two Hamburg translations and the first volume of Denis, which latter he reviewed, censuring its use of hexameters. He himself had transcribed specimens into the free rhythms of Klopstock, which he felt was the most appropriate available poetic form. He was, therefore, acquainted with only half of Ossian and vaguely informed about Ossianic criticism. His 'return to nature', however, on his sea-journey, with the upheaval in his outlook and plans, assured Ossian a place within his study of universal history as well as in his study of primitive poetry. In France he read translations and criticisms, by Diderot, Turgot, and Suard, all appreciative of Macpherson's poems as illustrating a primitive natural age. Then came the night of shipwreck and the reading of *Fingal* in an atmosphere of unique solemnity. In view of Herder's own emotional ferment and his imperfect and second-hand knowledge of the bard, it is clear that it was an idealized vision of Ossian that he enjoyed. He himself has explained how his vaulting imagination caused him always to see shadows instead of realities and how every impression assumed 'Gothic' proportions in his mind, and it is certain that his vision of Ossian, whose emotions corresponded so closely to his own and who possessed so strong a literary and historical appeal, was one that was highly romanticized, with something mystic, inscrutable, and incalculable about it.

The receipt of the two remaining volumes of Denis in Amsterdam was useful but disappointing. He had now the complete Ossian before him, although in an unsuitable metrical form. In the emotional excitement that followed his meeting with Caroline Flachsland, the poet's sentimental attraction was doubled. He frequently discussed him in letters to her, enclosing specimens, culled from Denis and touched up by himself, which were long held to be original translations. The meeting with Goethe in Strassburg and the penetration into English literature—Herder said that he became 'more and more British' at this time—was a break before the unending solitude and seclusion of Bückeburg. Here in his dejection he steeped himself in Ossian and nearly always carried a volume with him as he wandered in the surrounding woods. In this atmosphere of aching melancholy and unfulfilled longings he wrote his Ossian-essay in late July and in August, 1771, still with an Ossian of his own imagination in his mind. He never knew him in his real form until November—*after* the essay was finished and sent to press—when Goethe lent him his father's copy of the English text. He had judged by translations which he thought were more misleading than they really were, and built up his picture from what he knew or thought he knew of primitive poetry in general. It is significant that after this he began to talk more and more of the 'original' Gaelic. Goethe, in addition to sending him the text, submitted one or two passages which he had hacked out of Macpherson's 'specimen' of the Gaelic, together with comments of his own casting doubts on the value of the English version. The programme of the *Sturm und Drang* naturalism thus grew out of a romanticized vision that was based upon the most uncertain data. But the manifesto was out. The movement was in being.

It has been noted that Ossian had been used in Herder's campaign against Classical authority. Herder had at first linked him with the *Edda*, confusing Celts and Scandinavians, as Klopstock had done. Whatever were the real facts about the Celts, here was an example that greatly assisted his contention that poetry was a universal gift and not the monopoly of any one people—an example that was freely acknowledged to be the equal of Homer. So that it was henceforth impossible to go on arguing 'as if there were no bards and Scots in the world', as Herder put it. Ossian's strangeness inevitably drew attention to national peculiarities, and soon Herder began to characterize poetry from this new angle. Similarly, Ossian's authority was brought into the fray against Lessing's theory, based on Homer alone, that action and not description was the real subject of poetry. Ossian was held in greater regard because he possessed all the virtues ascribed to primitive literature. His example, by a natural twist in the thought process, was then quoted in support of these same qualities. The famous antithesis of 'nature-poetry' and 'art-poetry' quickly came to be the major theme of Herder's criticism. The Ossian-essay developed it and intensified it.

It must not be assumed that Ossian was the ultimate cause of Herder's poetic theory and of his interest in the folksong. The basis of these was evident in his earliest writings. Herder himself is emphatic on this point, and his wife explained that the Bible was the source of his enthusiasm for popular poetry. To this he added his acquaintance with Lettish folksongs. After his sea-journey he wrote:

'Aber auch das (i.e. the shipwreck) ist noch nicht eigentlich Genesis des Enthusiasmus, über welchen Sie mir Vorwürfe machen: denn sonst wäre er vielleicht nichts als individuelles Blendwerk, ein bloßes Meergespenst. Wissen Sie also, daß ich selbst Gelegenheit gehabt, lebendige Reste dieses alten, wilden Gesanges, Rhythmus, Tanzes, unter lebenden Völkern zu

sehen, denen unsre Sitten noch nicht völlig Sprache und Lieder und Ge-
bräuche haben nehmen können, um ihnen dafür etwas sehr Verstüm-
meltes oder nichts zu geben.'[1]

From these beginnings, his interest in the bard and his theory of
poetry developed hand in hand. Ossian stimulated and illustrated
opinions that were already growing, clinching a point here, suggesting
a new one there. The appeal was immense, and Ossian momentarily
became the archtype of primitive poet. His very vagueness was an
attraction, though it interfered with the application of Herder's
critical method—for how could he explain Ossian from a study of the
conditions of his time as he was wont to do, when next to nothing
was known about it and the poems themselves were almost devoid of
concrete fact?

It was natural for Herder to link Ossian with Percy's *Reliques*.
These had been made known in Germany in 1765 by Raspe, but
played no part in Herder's works until after he borrowed Raspe's
copy in August, 1771. His interest was meantime stimulated by an
extract from one of Percy's essays which he had read in France. The
Ossian-essay, finished immediately after he received the *Reliques*,
stands partly under their auspices. His appreciation of Ossian leads
to a defence of popular poetry and thence to a concluding challenge
to Germany to seek out her own folksongs.

A good deal of Herder's vehemence is due directly to two causes.
On the one hand he was horrified by Gerstenberg's deference to the
doubts that had been raised regarding the authenticity of Ossian. On
the other hand, the disappointment he felt at the hexameter version
of Denis knew no bounds, and he was not the man to hold his peace
at such a violation of the elemental and un-epic spirit of the poet.
His review of the last two volumes of Denis completely obliterated
the well-meaning translator with a torrent of furious invective. The
opinion that Ossian was lyric rather than epic was encouraged in
Herder by the knowledge that the poems of 1760 had been woven
into the longer pieces, as well as by some dark hints in Macpherson's
prefaces that he had occasionally welded fragments into larger units.
Herder, who had long assumed the lyrical origin of the epic, as indeed
of all poetry, could doubt no longer. When Percy's *Reliques* reached

[1] V. 169-170; 'But even that (i.e. the shipwreck) is not really the genesis of the enthusiasm
with which you reproach me; for if it were, it might perhaps be no more than an individual
illusion of mine, a mere phantom of the sea. You must know, therefore, that I have myself had
occasion to see living relics of this old, wild mode of song, rhythm and dance, among living
peoples, whom our customs have not yet fully deprived of their language, lays and usages in
return for something very mutilated or nothing at all.'

him, every shadow was dispelled. Now, everything was *Volkslied*, or *Nationallied*. Even the Creation story in the Book of Genesis could be shown to have developed out of a number of primitive folksongs. Herder isolated 'ballads' 'Von der Schöpfung der Welt', 'Vom Sabbat', 'Vom Verderben der Welt', and looked upon these as Hebrew poetical romances, akin to the folksongs of Percy or the supposed lyrical origins of Ossian. So absorbed was he in this thought that he even re-wrote these original Hebrew ballads in what he felt to be *the* characteristic folksong form, the Chevy Chase strophe. No wonder he could speak of 'Edward' and the 'Brudermord Kains' in the same breath!

Hence, whatever Macpherson or any one else might have done, Ossian was really lyric, *Lied*, the spontaneous outburst of nature speaking through an unconsciously creative genius.

'Aber das ist er nun nicht (i.e. epic), und sehen Sie, das wollte ich Ihnen nur sagen, von jenem (i.e. Ossian in hexameters) hat schon, wie mich dünkt, eine Kritische Bibliothek geredet, und das geht mich nichts an. Ihnen wollte ich nur in Erinnerung bringen, daß Ossians Gedichte *Lieder, Lieder des Volks, Lieder* (Herder's italics) eines ungebildeten sinnlichen Volks sind, die sich so lange im Munde der väterlichen Tradition haben fortsingen können—sind sie das in unsrer schönen epischen Gestalt gewesen? haben sies sein können?'[1]

As the essay proceeded, Herder unfolded his theory of the spontaneous origin of poetry. Not only Ossian, but Percy, Shakespeare, Lapp songs, Eskimo elegies, children's rhymes, even the Greeks themselves, were made to illustrate this contention. They all possessed the boldness and abruptness, the vividness and figurativeness of the popular style. Such were the qualities belonging to poetry produced in the time before art came and extinguished nature, and it was in such that Herder found German literature to be so woefully lacking. Salvation could not come about unless the *naiveté* and directness, the natural and unforced inspiration of the folksong were recaptured and drawn upon and developed. Herder was himself so keenly aware of these characteristics because of his remarkable power of transferring himself in spirit into other times and places—indeed as far as Ossian was concerned, he was infinitely more Ossianic than Ossian himself, more Celtic than the Celts!

---

[1] V. 160; 'But that is just what he is not (i.e. epic), and that is just what I wanted to say to you; I believe some critical periodical has already spoken about that (i.e. Ossian in hexameters), and I am not concerned with it. I merely wanted to remind you that Ossian's poems are songs, folksongs, songs of an uncultured, emotional people, which have sung their way down the ages on the lips of native tradition. Is that what they have been in our fine epic form? Have they ever been able to be that?'

The folksongs were ready at every one's hand. They only needed to be collected.

'In mehr als einer Provinz sind mir Volkslieder, Provinziallieder, Bauer-lieder bekannt, die an Lebhaftigkeit und Rhythmus, und Naivetät und Stärke der Sprache vielen derselben (i.e. Percy's) gewiß nichts nachgeben würden; nur wer ist der sie sammle? der sich um sie bekümmere? sich um Lieder des Volks bekümmere? auf Straßen und Gassen und Fischmärkten? im ungelehrten Rundgesange des Landvolks? um Lieder, die oft nicht skandiert und oft schlecht gereimt sind? wer wollte sie sammeln—wer für unsre Kritiker, die ja so gut Silben zählen und skandieren können, drucken lassen?'[1]

Herder pressed for their collection in order that German literature might become conscious of itself. The songs of the past, embodying national traditions, sentiments, and interests, must be the foundation for the future, not the no longer valid authority of Greece and Rome. Other literatures were the products of an undisturbed evolu-tion, whereas the course of German letters, as he declared in the essay 'Von Ähnlichkeit der mittleren englischen und deutschen Dicht-kunst' (1776), had been interruped by the foreign influence which the Renaissance had introduced. The only remedy, as Herder said so often, lay in resuming where the national tradition had broken off, i.e. in going back to the literature of the Middle Ages. The folksong was the link in which the native medieval tradition lived on. German poetry could only proceed on its own lines when it had taken the trouble to ascertain what these were. That was the method other countries had followed; and they had achieved greatness.

The fragment on Shakespeare—for the discussion breaks off just when it is approaching the heart of the problem—is a natural corol-lary. It is a striking example of the successful application of the historical method of criticism. Herder's chameleon-like self-surrender to the colour and spirit of the times and places under discussion leads to a new and highly fertile evaluation of the Greek, French, and English drama in their relations to one another. By looking at them historically, he quickly concludes that they each possess a relative and not an absolute validity.

Herder's knowledge of Shakespeare was almost as defective as

---

[1] V. 189; 'In more than one province folksongs, dialect songs, peasant songs are known to me, which would certainly yield in no wise to many of those (of Percy) as regards animation, and rhythm, and *naiveté* and strength of language. Only who is there who will collect them, who will trouble himself about them, trouble himself about songs of the people, in the streets and alleys and fishmarkets, in the unlearned glee-parties of the peasant-folk, songs which often do not scan and which rhyme badly? Who would be willing to collect them, who would have them printed for the benefit of our critics, who as we know can count syllables and scan so well?'

his knowledge of Ossian. He relied primarily on Wieland's translation, which presented a misleading picture, in that it stressed the
romantic aspect and, by reason of its being mainly in prose, gave an
exaggerated impression of freedom and lawlessness in the original;
while the notes Wieland gave made many feel that here was a case of a
bungler wrestling with the work of a great genius. Until 1769, when
he acquired Johnson's edition (which reprinted the prefaces of previous editors), probably only *Hamlet* and possibly *Macbeth* were at
all well known to Herder in English.

Herder had two important predecessors in Shakespearean criticism
in Germany, Gerstenberg and Lessing. The former was a man of
impressions and preferred to point out what appealed to him, rather
than to judge by any aesthetic norms. Whereas Gerstenberg stressed
Shakespeare's creativeness and power as an interpreter of human life,
Lessing merely regarded the English poet as a rod to use on French
Classicism, by maintaining that he had fulfilled the true purpose of
tragedy, as set out by Aristotle—that of *katharsis*—better than the
French, though they knew the rules of Aristotle and he did not. The
implication in this was that to attain the proper purpose of tragedy
was more important than to observe rule and precept.

The heart of Herder's interpretation—his *Lieblingsidee*—was that
Shakespeare had used popular ballads and traditions, folksongs and
romances, as the bases of his work, indeed that his whole
achievement grew out of such origins.

'Wie? auf welche Kunst und Schöpferweise Shakespear eine elende
Romanze, Novelle, Fabelhistorie zu solch einem lebendigen Ganzen habe
dichten können?... Wie hat Shakespear aus Romanzen und Novellen
Drama gedichtet?'[1]

These were the key problems he set out to solve. It was indeed the
folksong, as Herder's widow said, that developed his affection for
Shakespeare, as for Ossian. As his view of the folksong widened, so
did his vision of Shakespeare move towards its culmination. Accordingly, the loan of Percy's *Reliques* from Raspe in August, 1771, not
only rendered possible the completion of the Ossian essay, but also
brought his ideas on Shakespeare to fruition. Just as the epic, Homer
as well as Ossian, had originated in the songs and rhapsodies of
minstrels, later fused together into coherent units, so the plays of
Shakespeare were the outcome of similar ballad materials, i.e. drama-

---

[1] V. 229; 'How, in what artistic and creative manner, could Shakespeare transform a miserable ballad, story, or myth into such a living whole? How did Shakespeare compose drama from
ballads and stories?'

tizations of lyrical romances. Significant remarks of Johnson, Theobald, and Warton supported this theory—such as 'his English histories he took from English chronicles and English ballads', or 'historical songs, then very fashionable, often suggested and recommended a subject. Many of his incidental allusions also relate to pieces of this kind. . . . A ballad is still remaining on the subject of Romeo and Juliet, which by the date appears to be much older than Shakespeare's time'; or 'I doubt not but he received the hint of writing on King Lear from a ballad of that subject'. The *Reliques*, which contained a whole section entitled 'Ballads that illustrate Shakespeare'—'ballads quoted by Shakespeare or (which) contribute in any degree to illustrate his writings', 'our great dramatic poet having occasionally quoted ancient ballads, and even taken the plot of one, if not more of his plays from among them'—provided vital documentary evidence.

No wonder Herder called for a collection of German folksongs so insistently in the Ossian-essay! As he said in connection with his own anthology of 1778-9, folksongs could be regarded more as providing materials for poetry than as themselves poetry—though the qualification seems a little unjust to their intrinsic merit from the pen of the supreme champion of the folksong. That is why he urged Goethe to collect specimens in Alsace with such vigour. They might be used, as was 'Come away, Come away, Death'—sung by 'the spinsters and the knitters in the sun'—and many another with which he was familiar in the plays of Shakespeare. Of the ballads Goethe collected, eight were concerned with the subject of the faithless lover, and, whatever other elements added themselves to the Gretchen-story in the *Urfaust*, the folksong origin of that story is amply apparent; and when it is remembered that the *Urfaust* based itself upon the folk-drama and puppet play, still in vogue in Goethe's youth, quite apart from its ultimate chapbook source, we see that the whole drama was constructed entirely out of popular origins—it was dramatized folk-song and folk-chronicle and elevated folk-drama, quite in the Shakespearean tradition as presented by Herder. In exactly the same way, Goethe took the tragic ending of *Clavigo* from an Alsatian folksong about a faithless lover. Similarly he turned to the autobiography of Götz von Berlichingen, another instance of a native chronicle, belonging to an age when the natural development of German literature was still undeflected by foreign influence. For the same reason, too, songs and ballads are inserted in his plays, in the Shakespearean manner, such as 'Es war ein König in Thule', 'Es war eine Ratt' im Kellernest' in the *Urfaust*, 'Es fing ein Knab' ein Vögelein' in *Götz*, 'Freudvoll und leidvoll' in *Egmont*, all in the folksong mode and following the example of 'Under the Greenwood Tree', 'Willow, willow, willow', and others, while the open discussion of the folksong in *Claudine von Villa Bella* makes Goethe's adhesion to Herder's teaching even more obvious.

A German Shakespeare could, therefore, be born only of the German folksong. If only German literature had been able to grow out of and build upon the poetic material of the Middle Ages, as English literature had done, Herder would not have had to lay about him so drastically and plead so vehemently. For Percy's essays and Dodsley's introduction to his *Collection of Old Plays* (1744), as well as Johnson's authoritative observations, revealed Shakespeare to him as the heir of the ballad-mongers and strolling minstrels, so that there was clearly, in his eyes, a regular line of descent from the scalds and bards of ancient times to the peak of the Elizabethan drama and beyond. Ossian and Shakespeare were thus very significantly juxtaposed in his little collection of *Fliegende Blätter*.

Besides drawing so abundantly and fruitfully upon the folksong tradition, Shakespeare himself became part of it. The story of the genesis of the first folio, culled from many scattered sources and often taken down from actual stage performances, as Theobald declared, corresponded as nearly as might be to Herder's theories on the origin of the Homeric epics, which he regarded as composite works based upon lyrical fragments. Might not Shakespeare's minstrelsy be dramatic, as that of Homer was lyrical? Had not Herder already insisted upon the dramatic element as a characteristic of the ballad? Further, Shakespeare's lyrical snatches in the folksong mode, such as 'Full fathom five' and others, merged so indistinguishably with this mode that Shakespeare well deserved the title of *Volksdichter*. All his work illustrated in a most compelling manner the course in which a literature should progress, the very course which had been denied to Germany, so disastrously and irreparably. This is at the foundation of Herder's important historical comparison of the Greek, French, and English drama which fills the major part of the Shakespeare-fragment as we know it.

In this, Herder stresses national distinctions. To attempt to reproduce the Greek drama, which belonged to Greek civilization, or to apply its rules, in the entirely different environment of France, was in his eyes utterly absurd, and he said so. The English drama, on the other hand, bore a major resemblance to the Greek. It was independent and original, imitating nothing outside itself, having a native origin and a native purpose. Shakespeare was a poet of the people, expressing its thoughts and sentiments; his work was a development of elementary folksong beginnings just as that of Sophocles was. The reference to Shakespeare as the brother of Sophocles was therefore no mere empty repetition of Young's dictum. In the parallel, however, was to be found also a difference, and this marks one of Herder's most acute contributions to comparative criticism. Whereas the Greek drama evolved complexity out of simple origins, the English moved forward towards simplicity from complexity. Each had its own characteristics and justification, and so might any other literature have that was unfettered and loyal to its own genius. For poetic inspiration was universal. Hence the encouraging greeting to the author of *Götz von Berlichingen* at the end of the essay, whose work might begin a renaissance of German literature that might rival the achievements of the age of Elizabeth.

Actual dramaturgical matters are of small importance beside these ideas, though Herder has significant observations to make, in passing, concerning such topical subjects as the Unities, Aristotle's *katharsis*, illusion, characterization, and scenic effect. To all of these the historical approach is the only one of which Herder is capable. It should not be assumed that he was indifferent to such things, or that he considered Shakespeare as a poet whose works were to be read rather than to be seen acted.

Herder's attitude to Shakespeare's genius was of revolutionary importance. That original genius was something divine or possessed was, of course, not a novel opinion. But Herder did not stop at that. Genius was for him part of the very mechanism of the universe, which used him as its mouthpiece to proclaim its message to mankind. When he designated Shakespeare, therefore, as *Schöpfer, Göttersohn, dramatischer Gott*, he was employing no rhetorical figure of speech; he meant exactly what he said—that Shakespeare was more than divinely inspired; that he was god-like, a creator in miniature, whose work followed and illustrated the same processes as Creation itself. Creation is not a thing that has been completed once and for all; it is continuous, going on everywhere before our very eyes, and nature is a living and a growing whole. All history is the record of this process. Its agents are the great geniuses of the world, the 'heroes' in Carlyle's sense. The poet's function is to make known God's purpose; to interpret nature or the universe, of which he is a part, by making it live again, by reconstructing and reproducing its modes of operation, by re-creating it, as it were, before the eyes and ears of his

E

fellow-men, so that they may perceive and comprehend its workings. His part is accordingly akin to that of the educator or evangelist, leading men, by virtue of his superior gifts and insight, to see and follow out the preordained plan of the world. This was actually what Shakespeare taught Herder himself to do, as will be seen.

'Wie vor einem Meere von Begebenheit,wo Wogen in Wogen rauschen, so tritt vor seine Bühne. Die Auftritte der Natur rücken vor und ab; wirken ineinander, so disparat sie scheinen; bringen sich hervor und zerstören sich, damit die Absicht des Schöpfers, der alle im Plane der Trunkenheit und Unordnung (a dig at Voltaire!) gesellt zu haben schien, erfüllt werde—dunkle kleine Symbole zum Sonnenriß einer Theodizee Gottes. . . . Eine Welt dramatischer Geschichte, so groß und tief wie die Natur; aber der Schöpfer gibt uns Auge und Gesichtspunkt, so groß und tief zu sehen!' [1]

Shakespearean drama, then, is fundamentally an interpretation of the world. Shakespeare dramatizes history—but not merely in the ordinary sense of writing historical plays. With all its powerful illusion of actuality, his work is akin to Revelation itself. When Herder states, therefore, that he loses all idea of theatre and wings and actors when reading Shakespeare—a statement that has given rise to all kinds of absurd opinions, e.g. that he regarded Shakespeare as a lyricist—he means merely this, that his attention is monopolized by the manifestation of the world-process with which he is presented— the 'Blätter aus dem Buch der Begebenheiten, der Vorsehung, der Welt'.[2] It is thus clear why Shakespeare, with Homer and Ossian, is linked with Moses, Mahomet, and Prometheus in Herder's mind. Creative genius is not exclusively poetical.

A more forceful way of encouraging German Shakespeares could hardly have been found than this. Herder's discovery of the cosmic meaning of poetry inspired the new movement in Germany with a deep sense of the greatness, even sublimity, of its purpose. The *Sturm und Drang* could go on its way confident that it had a mission to fulfil. But the dangers inherent in such excessive self-consciousness have affected German literature ever since.

---

[1] V. 220-1; 'His stage comes forth, as it were, from out of a whole ocean of action, where wave swirls into wave. The scenes of nature move to and fro, each affecting the other, however disparate they appear to be. They are mutually creative and destructive, so that the intention of the creator, who appears to have juxtaposed them in no other scheme than that of drunkenness and disorder, may be fulfilled—they are small, dark symbols that contribute to an outline of a theodicy. . . . A whole world of dramatic history, as mighty and profound as nature herself. Only the creator gives us eyes to see and a standpoint, so that our vision may be just as mighty and profound.'

[2] V. 219; 'Leaves from the book of all action, of Providence, of the world.'

The *Volkslieder* of 1774 matured in the closest association with the study of Shakespeare and English literature. Indeed, this collection, unlike its successor of four years later, was restricted to specimens from England and Germany, and a whole section in it was devoted to the English dramatist. Herder, it may be said, applied himself to Shakespeare because he sprang from the folksong (not merely because he *was* folksong), and to the folksong because it illustrated Shakespeare; though this, of course, does not cover the whole extent of his interest. In his notes and prefaces to his anthology is to be found much of the material which Herder doubtless would have included in his Shakespeare-fragment, had he continued it and developed its *idée maîtresse*. The essay 'Von Ähnlichkeit der mittleren englischen und deutschen Dichtkunst', for instance, which was published in 1777 and is one of the most profound and significant of his contributions to criticism, attempts to explain why Germany, unlike England, had not had a Shakespeare despite the racial affinity and the mythology and language originally common to the two nations. While English literature based itself upon and drew from the popular substance of the Middle Ages, Germany, with kindred foundations, had not done so, and had indeed lost touch entirely with its primitive, native material. (It may be noted, by the way, that here was the origin of the German claim that Shakespeare, as the heir of the Teutonic minstrels, is a German poet!) Whereas in England the native poetic tradition was so strong as not to be deflected by the foreign substance of the Renaissance but rather to assimilate it and turn it to good purpose, a succession of events—namely the loss of Charles the Great's folksong collection, the Latin domination of German culture in the Middle Ages, followed by the Renaissance and Wars of Religion—had cheated German literature of its due, so weakened it as to make it subservient to French literature, and made an irreparable breach between the present and its own national past.

'Aus ältern Zeiten haben wir also durchaus keine lebende Dichterei, auf der unsre neuere Dichtkunst, wie Sprosse auf dem Stamm der Nation gewachsen wäre; dahingegen andre Nationen mit den Jahrhunderten fortgegangen sind, und sich auf eigenem Grunde, aus Nationalprodukten, auf dem Glauben und Geschmack des Volks, aus Resten alter Zeiten gebildet haben. Dadurch ist ihre Dichtkunst und Sprache national worden, Stimme des Volks ist genutzt und geschätzt, sie haben in diesen Dingen weit mehr ein Publikum bekommen, als wir haben. Wir arme Deutsche sind von jeher bestimmt gewesen, nie unser zu bleiben: immer die

Gesetzgeber und Diener fremder Nationen, ihre Schicksalsentscheider und ihre verkaufte, blutende, ausgesogene Sklaven.'[1]

Herder's angry envy could only point to Percy's example as the one to be followed, and he proceeded to illustrate it, with admirable skill both as selector and as translator, with his own anthology. His aim was to make available the lost treasures of the past as a foundation for future writers to build upon; to bring about in contemporary Germany a set of literary conditions similar to those of Elizabethan England, out of which new Shakespeares and Spensers might grow. That mockery and hostility caused the withdrawal of his collection from the press was a bitter blow to this *Lieblingsidee* of Herder's. The *Volkslieder* of 1778-9 did not reflect quite the same intention.

[1] IX. 528; 'Thus, from ancient times we have absolutely no living poetic literature upon which our modern poetry might grow, as a branch upon the national stem; whereas other nations have progressed with the centuries, and have shaped themselves upon their own soil, from native products, upon the belief and taste of the people, from the remains of the past. In that way their literature and language have become national, the voice of the people has been used and cherished, they have secured far more of a public in these matters than we Germans have. We poor Germans have been destined from the start never to remain ourselves; ever to be the lawgivers and servants of foreign nationalities, the directors of their fate and their bartered, bleeding, exhausted slaves.'

CHAPTER V

THE TRANSITION TO HISTORY

THE intensity of Herder's conviction that it was his task to study the character and development of the human soul soon became almost unendurable. His whole attitude towards history and literature was re-orientated. Hitherto he had explained poetry by means of history. Henceforth, without, however, discarding this purpose, he proceeded in the reverse direction, to explain history by means of literature. Literature is now a means to an end, not merely an end in itself. Its importance lies, as Herder said so often, in the guidance it gives towards an understanding of the human mind and its workings. It can supply information that might be otherwise unobtainable about mankind in past ages. Poetry thus becomes the handmaid of history.

This is the first phase in the evolution of Herder's thought. It was clear as early as the *Fragmente* that the two processes were so inextricably interlocked as to be often almost indistinguishable. One wonders whether Herder himself was at all times certain which one he was following out. For there were serious difficulties; and though logic and clarity were never his strong points, it is nevertheless obvious that his peace of mind was gravely disturbed by the feeling that something was wrong. This is no doubt the reason why so many of his works remained fragments. Obviously, to explain a piece of literature with the aid of history, and then at the same time to utilize that same piece of literature to throw light upon history, is coming perilously near to arguing in a circle. To avoid the danger was quite beyond Herder's powers. Evidently, the very widest vision and most comprehensive knowledge were necessary, or he would forever be condemned to the unhappy task of explaining one unknown in terms of another. Herder's despair was no less great than Faust's, and his search for a magic formula of release no less urgent.

Much significance has been attached to the influence of Rousseau in connection with Herder's historical sense, and—especially in view of his championship of nature and feeling—Herder has frequently been declared to be Rousseau's pupil. The affinity is unmistakable, yet to assign to Rousseau a determining significance is misleading. Though at first carried away with reckless enthusiasm, Herder, almost immedi-

ately, learned from Hume the chimerical nature of the golden age
of innocence and in the *Reisejournal* his judgement on Rousseau is
severe. Herder's apotheosis of the senses is sufficiently accounted for
by his own emotional character and by the preparatory instruction
of Hamann. Moreover, while agreeing with Rousseau's dislike of
contemporary culture, he was not content merely to gaze back
regretfully at an ideal past, but looked rather towards an ideal future,
that would be the outcome of all the forces of humanity properly
developed. What these forces were and what direction they should
take, it became his life's work to ascertain.

Moreover, his conception of nature had a deeper foundation.
Hamann's view of the world as a mighty symbol of the divine,
apprehensible only through the senses, grew into the idea of a
universe, filled with the spirit of God, progressively revealing Himself and completing His work through nature and man. History and
Revelation were thus identical. It followed that everything representing individuality of person or period or nation ought to be respected
as parts of this progressive Revelation, and that individuality of self-
expression should not be impeded by human conventions, but
cultivated and encouraged. (That to hinder individual self-expression
may equally be regarded as another aspect of this all-embracing
Revelation is inherent in this convenient argument, but does not seem
to have occurred to Herder.) The works of primitive peoples were
looked upon, therefore, not merely with beglamoured Rousseauistic
delight, but with something approximating to religious awe; for,
having no barriers between themselves and the inexhaustible sources
of Creation, they were found to show its workings the more clearly.

To consider poetic genius as possessing an apostolic nature was a
further inevitable consequence of this. In a striking passage Herder
wrote:

'Ein Dichter ist Schöpfer eines Volkes um sich: er gibt ihnen eine Welt
zu sehen und hat ihre Seelen in seiner Hand, sie dahin zu führen! . . . Wie
der Magnet das Eisen, kann er Herzen an sich ziehen und wie der elektrische
Funke allgegenwärtig durchdringt, allmächtig fortwandelt, so trifft auch
sein Blitz, wo er will, die Seele.'[1]

Literature in this way acquired for Herder both an historical and an
educative function. His explanation of history by means of poetry

---

[1] VIII. 433–4; 'A poet is the creator of a people around him; he gives his hearers a world to
look upon, and has their souls in his hands to lead them to it. Just as the magnet attracts iron,
so he can draw human hearts to himself, and just as the electric spark penetrates everywhere
and goes irresistibly on its way, so does the lightning of his message reach men's souls whereso-
ever he will.'

assumed a more and more profound significance, the more emphatic-
ally he realized this. He was convinced, as Shelley and Victor Hugo
and Carlyle were, that there was no essential difference between
poetry and prophecy.

'Dichtkunst', he had already declared, 'sie ist ursprünglich Theologie gewesen, und die edelste, höchste Dichtkunst wird wie die Tonkunst ihrem
Wesen nach immer Theologie bleiben. Sänger und Propheten, die erhaben-
sten Dichter des Alten Testaments schöpften Flammen aus heiligem Feuer.
Die ältesten ehrwürdigsten Dichter des Heidentums, Gesetzgeber, Väter
und Bilder der Menschen, Orpheus und Epimenodes und alle Fabelnamen
der Urzeit, sangen die Götter und beseligten die Welt.'[1]

Only in so far as it expressed the highest moral qualities, pure and
undefiled, did poetry earn his approval. Herder firmly subordinated
aesthetics to ethics, and he held to this standpoint to the end. It
followed, of course, that primitive poetry satisfied this requirement
per se. But in regard to contemporary poetry the matter was different.

In his antagonism to modern civilization and his proposals for its
improvement, literature occupied a leading position. It is at the
centre of all his thought. Yet the very possibility of its existence, in
any real form, such as he had advocated so earnestly, seemed ques-
tionable unless the laxity and corruption he saw in his own times could
be overcome and a general rejuvenation achieved. Poetry was not
only a producer of morality but its product too. Without great
poetry, then, how could the decadent age be moralized? And foreign
literature was expressly ruled out as a possible aid! Here was an
impasse indeed. The times themselves needed to be regenerated before
poetry could start on its moralizing task. In the teeth of an insoluble
problem, Herder flung himself into battle, with faith alone to sustain
him. He was at loggerheads with the world in any case. He made the
quarrel as violent as he could, and, in self-justification, found every
possible fault with the forces arrayed against him. For a start,
since the age had passed away when poetry was undistorted by
convention and was naturally an agent for good, he was prepared to
impose a censorship upon frivolity and licence, in order to ensure its
adhesion to the service of civilization. Evidently he had momentarily
forgotten his insistence upon spontaneity as the major element in
poetic production! Or perhaps it was merely a case of shifted empha-

---

[1] VII. 300; Poetry was originally theology, and the noblest and most elevated poetry will,
like music, always remain in essence theology. Singers and prophets, the sublimest poets of
the Old Testament derived flames from the holy fire. The oldest and most venerable heathen
poets, lawgivers, fathers and educators of mankind, Orpheus and Epimenodes and all the
fabulous names of early times, sang of the gods and gave rapture to the world.'

sis, for now it is the *effect* of literature that is uppermost in his thoughts rather than its causes.

It was in this perplexed frame of mind that he compiled the *Volkslieder* of 1778-9 and planned a further anthology just before he died. His vision had indeed widened considerably since the ill-fated collection of 1774. He pierces through the songs he quotes to the nations that produced them, and through these to the very depths of human nature itself and its sources of creativeness. The limited number of German specimens in his collection is sufficiently accounted for by his universality of outlook, although the compiler was, at the same time, disappointed by the poor yield, as well as disgusted by the unholy rowdiness manifested for and against his folksong programme. It was not that his literary patriotism had diminished, despite his rejection of the title of a German Percy; it merely operated from a different angle. He felt now that the best way to cultivate German self-consciousness was to show his country its place among the other peoples of the world. Examples from all literatures are therefore included in his anthology, even from as far away as Greenland and Peru. Ossian, who was a sort of godfather to the first collection, is represented by three specimens only, two of them translated from the 'original Gaelic', and is passed over in conspicuous silence in the prefaces; for Herder had received important evidence against the authenticity and was unwilling to commit himself very far in either direction. The *Volkslieder* constitute *the* single work by which Herder has been generally remembered, though it is forgotten how very many well-known poems owe their popularity to his enterprise. His German renderings are a permanent memorial to his uncanny power of transporting himself into the spirit of other times and nations and to the delicacy of his poetic sensibility. All later anthologies by German compilers were in his debt, and the study of *Weltliteratur* by Goethe and the early Romantic school was prepared by his practical example.

In the final transition from literature to history the Shakespeare experience was the second and decisive stage. As soon as Herder strove to understand the age from which Shakespeare sprang and to understand Shakespeare as a means of understanding his age, he became in intention, if not in execution, an historian, or something more. That was precisely what happened when he considered England, France, and Ancient Greece in their relationship to one another. It was not criticism or comparative literature alone that he wrote. It was the beginning of the philosophy of history.

Shakespeare led Herder to history. As the culmination of the Middle Ages, he at once induced that romanticization of the Middle Ages and of their piety, heroism, and sentiment that graces the pages of *Auch Eine Philosophie der Geschichte*. But he worked also in a more profound way. Seeing history 'dramatized' by Shakespeare, Herder himself looked upon it as a great drama. He saw the interconnection of scenes and characters, all subservient to the one ultimate purpose set by God, a purpose which may not indeed be perceptible to those participating, but which nevertheless exists. Just as Shakespeare was a kind of miniature creator, so God could be looked upon as a kind of super-dramatist, and the world as a stage.

Here was a working plan for Herder's developing ideas on the philosophy of history. To be sure it was an artist's plan rather than a philosopher's and was reached by feeling rather than argument, but at least it provided a habitation for those formless abstractions that filled his mind. He learned to see movement and continuity in history as in some gigantic tragedy constructed by an omnipotent and omniscient Providence. Naturally this was a fatalistic view; all things, while developing in their own ways—being true to themselves, like characters in a play—are ultimately merely links in the chain of progress towards a preordained goal. It only remained to discover what this goal was, or at least how the key to it could be found.

Thus, Herder's vision of history is in origin an expansion of his literary criticism. A secure foundation, upon which his new idea could build, was provided by religion. This is the final stage. Very soon theology swallowed up history and made it part of itself. It was all theology before long, so quickly did events move in Herder's mind. Religion completed the all-embracing re-orientation of his thought. To explain literature out of history and history out of literature had been, so far, little better than evaluating x in terms of y and y in terms of x. Now, in religion, he had a constant central factor to which all things might be related. He could set about the execution of his grandiose plans of the *Reisejournal*. The idea of growth and development that had occupied him in literature could now be profitably transferred to history.

Herder's renewed study of the Bible began in Bückeburg and reached its greatest intensity in the company of the Countess Maria. It was encouraged and given heightened significance by an absorption in the *Pensées* of Pascal, which, we are told, were always on his table. Pascal's effect was to crystallize into manageable form Herder's maturing views upon religion, to fertilize and guide his growing convictions. Herder found in the *Pensées* what he was thinking and could not express. Their sober and precise reasoning gave cohesion to his own extravagant musings and assisted him to find a means of setting them down. He found in Pascal an ally in his self-imposed task of defeating the rationalist and academic pedants, of cleansing religion from the corrosive influences of the professional commentators, and of restoring that harmony between the world and the will of God, the loss of which he saw increasingly clearly to be the origin of the spiritual degeneration of the day.

Pascal may be regarded as a second Hamann for Herder—and it is noteworthy that the renewal of Hamann's influence, after a minor estrangement of some three years, coincides with this fresh return to religion. He asserted what Hamann had stressed so vigorously, the primacy of the senses over reason. 'C'est le coeur qui suit Dieu et non la raison.' Feeling, intuition, and faith—'le coeur'—these are the only true sources of knowledge, as of religion. Hence Pascal's constant intonation of the Psalmist's prayer for faith to be given, 'Inclina cor meum, Deus'. Nature operates for reasons of which reason is unaware; reason can itself demonstrate its own limitations, and may be used for any purpose the will decrees; the heart has its reasons that reason does not know; instinct and experience alone instruct man concerning all his being; the heart, not reason, gives us knowledge of first principles, which reason distorts once it begins to explain them. The way to God lies through the senses, and God is the source of all knowledge. If God did not tell us, we should not know what it is necessary for us to know, and we should be helpless to guide our existence. He may only be apprehended by the senses that are attuned and the heart that believes. All this, presented with impeccable lucidity, must have been more than revealing to the pupil of Hamann. In Pascal Herder discovered what he himself had been dreaming of as the new foundation of knowledge and religion. His shipwreck had converted him to an unshakable belief in feeling and faith as the channels through which God could be approached; and the solitide and gloom of life in Bückeburg forced him more and more into the consoling arms of religion. He accepted God as the first principle of all, and Revelation as a fact of incontrovertible reality.

This was the real basis of Herder's history. The immediate task was to study the first Revelation of all, as recorded in the Bible. All he would need to do, then, would be to use history to illustrate it. The Book of Genesis, the oldest document of mankind, must, therefore, as a necessary preliminary, be made to yield up its secret. The riddle of human life must be read from God's intervention at the start. Herder addressed himself to the task of understanding the Old Testament full of the positive aggressiveness with which Faust approached the New, and of the feeling that without God, without Revelation, we can know nothing, and without faith we cannot even know God. His own Biblical studies, like his history, were primarily an act of faith. The single-hearted devoutness that he demanded of others, he achieved first within himself.

In another way Herder now found his own thoughts much easier to follow, thanks to his reading of Pascal. He could see how Pascal made use of the method of immanence, without accepting the doctrine of immanence—which was, indeed, what he himself did. Nature and God are for him not co-extensive. Nature is no more than a living symbol, the 'garment', while God is the all-sustaining, inscrutable Creator. Nature declares the glory of God to those who believe, and it is for His Kingdom, the hereafter, that man is intended. It is true that there are times when Herder seems to approach the pantheistic position—he himself perhaps realized it— and this is the source of the confusion that has dogged his interpreters, and of much of the disharmony he himself was aware of in his own outlook. Yet there is nothing in the writings of these or other years to suggest that he was any other than a believer in a transcendental God. Although, it is true, some relics of medieval scholasticism, together with the effects of the philosophy of Leibniz, seem to suggest a disposition towards belief in immanence, it is clear that it was only the outer framework of this doctrine that he adopted, adding it, as it were, to his orthodoxy as a supplementary factor.

Herder thus had now both the purpose and the perspective for his historical survey. It merely remained for him to extract the message the Bible provided, and the way would be clear. The Bible taught that the source and the end of all things was God. It was, therefore, only necessary to know all that could be known about that source and end. Formerly Herder's approach to the Bible, in the Riga days, had been almost entirely aesthetic and literary. He had regarded the Old Testament, following upon the findings of Lowth, as Hebrew literature, the character of which was determined by the particular circumstances in which it flourished. This was the spirit in which the *Archäologie des Morgenlandes* was conceived. Afterwards, Herder had himself learned to feel the sustaining power of God and to realize that God creating is God revealing Himself. His attitude to the Bible changed then to a religious attitude. The *Älteste Urkunde des Men-*

schengeschlechts regarded it not only as poetry but as Revelation. The Book of Genesis was for Herder now not only Eastern poetry but the oldest document of the race. To study it was more than a mere archaeological exercise. It was the one and only guide to the comprehension of human life, exceeding in value all the speculations of all the philosophers. This was in accord with the teachings of Hamann, to whom Herder wrote:

'Glauben Sie, mein liebster Freund, es wird einst werden, daß die Offenbarung und Religion Gottes, statt daß sie jetzt Kritik und Politik ist, simple Geschichte und Weisheit unsres Geschlechts werde. Die magre Bibel wird alle 7 Wissenschaften der Alten, und 1000 der Neuen Welt, wie die fetten Kühe Pharaons in sich schlucken—dann wird sich aber die Not erst anheben—bis ein Tag kommt, der durch Facta und Acta Alles entsiegelt. Glücklich, von fern dazu vorbereitet, verkündigt, beigetragen zu haben. Ich bin nun einmal *der* Wissenschaften Diener, aber treulich will ich ihnen dienen.'[1]

So ran Herder's ringing confession of faith in his own undertaking. His method—the genetical method—was the one he had always followed. He accepted, like Pascal, the historicity of the Creation story. The source of all effort is God. All civilization derives from His Creation and from His instruction of man. Creation is made understandable through the sight of the Dawn, its ever-recurring symbol, which, if only man is attuned and believes, can teach what it has always taught, the life, the order, and the purpose within the universe. Further, Herder asserted that God revealed to man a mystic, all-expressive sign, a hieroglyph whose basis is the human shape, representing in visual and mnemonic form the meaning of the cosmos. This sign is a hexagon with a central point, symbolizing each of the Creation days, and Herder claimed to have discovered modifications of it in all primitive oriental cultures. He declared it to be the oldest poetical image of the universe and the origin of all knowledge and wisdom, of all myth and philosophy, of all language and poetry.

Herder shows at this time more than a little affinity with Faust. The desire to grasp the whole of life and the universe and to set forth its meaning, so as 'die Menschen zu bessern und zu bekehren',[2] is an

---

[1] *Briefe an Hamann*, p. 80; 'Believe me, my dearest friend, the time will come, when Revelation and religion, instead of being matters of criticism and politics, as they are now, will be the simple story and wisdom of our race. The thin Bible will swallow up all the seven arts of the ancient world and a thousand of the modern world, as if they were the fat kine of Pharaoh—then indeed will begin tribulation—until the day comes that will unseal all things by actual acts and deeds. Happy the man who from afar off has prepared, announced and assisted this. I am indeed the servant of those arts, but right loyally will I serve them.'

[2] *Faust*, 373; 'To help or convert a fellow-creature.' (*Faust* quotations are in Bayard Taylor's translation unless otherwise stated.)

obvious point of similarity. The urge to be more than an idle spectator and to intervene actively in the course of things, the markedly sensualistic and irrationalist cast of his thought, the positive, reckless pugnacity, these also at once spring to mind. There are points of detail, even verbal echoes, that show how closely Goethe was affected by this aspect of his friend's work. The impulse to flee into the arms of nature from the pedantry and futility of book-learning is followed in the case of both men by the imperious demand for the teachings of Revelation, nature alone without the necessary key to its understanding being unsatisfying. Revelation is to supply what the sciences alone cannot yield. Without knowledge of the Creator's intentions, the world—the past—as Faust tells Wagner, is a book with seven seals, which we cannot help misunderstanding as we are bound to read our own ideas into it. But once we have grasped God's intentions, in so far as they are perceptible in the origin of things, then we shall see God at all times, in all places, in all nature, His 'living garment'.

'Welch reine erhabne Art des Vortrags! kein Wort, kein Befehl, kein Rat —nur stilles Vorbild, Tat; aber die Tat, das Vorbild ist Gottes, geht vom Himmel zur Erde, durchströmt die ganze Natur der Welt und des Menschen.'[1]

These and similar passages—and there are many—may profitably be read in conjunction with the Earth-Spirit's self-characterization in *Faust*. Of the fullness and harmony of the universe the macrocosm-sign—Herder's hexagon—is the symbol. The very *sight* of it fills Faust with new strength and joy—rather as the sight of the sun enthralls the archangels in the 'Prologue in Heaven'—for he can see and understand the living, never-ending, concordant activity that streams through all things. His longing is stilled, and his words:

> Ich schau in diesen reinen Zügen
> Die wirkende Natur vor meiner Seele liegen.
> Jetzt erst erkenn' ich was der Weise spricht:
> 'Die Geisterwelt ist nicht verschlossen,
> Dein Sinn ist zu, dein Herz ist tot!
> Auf, bade, Schüler, unverdrossen
> Die irdische Brust im Morgenrot!'[2]

---

[1] VI. 286; 'What a pure, sublime mode of speech! Not words, nor commands, nor counsel—merely a silent symbol, action; only the action, the symbol is God's, comes from heaven to earth, and permeates the whole nature of the world and of men.'

[2] *Faust*, 440 ff.; 'In these pure features I behold
Creative Nature to my soul unfold.
What says the sage, now first I recognize:
"The spirit-world no closures fasten;
Thy sense is shut, thy heart is dead:
Disciple, up! untiring hasten
To bathe thy breast in morning-red!"'

contain an unmistakable verbal echo of the *Urkunde* as well as an allusion to the symbolic significance of the Dawn. 'Der Weise' can be none other than Herder. It is known, from a letter to Schönborn of 1774, how great an effect the *Urkunde* had upon Goethe at the very time he was at work upon the *Urfaust*.

The *Älteste Urkunde* may justly be regarded as the dominating work of Herder's Bückeburg period. All his other writings, including *Auch Eine Philosophie* and even the literary essays in *Von Deutscher Art und Kunst*, only acquire their full significance when read in the light of its findings. Its mysticism is continued in *Maran Atha*, which strove to interpret the Book of Revelation. It was inevitable, too, that Herder should demand a more natural and less academic outlook in the pastoral calling, such as he defined in his *Provinzialblätter* and *Briefe, das Studium der Theologie betreffend*. But it was in his sermons that the clearest statement of his position may be found, for in them, addressed as they were to a peasant congregation, he was compelled to express his beliefs with directness and simplicity. The existence of a divine purpose in the world, which is inscrutable and cannot be fully revealed until the end; the activity of God throughout all nature; the demand that life should obey the divine laws of nature, and fulfil the powers that have been given to it; the condemnation of sin as unnaturalness, or a falling-away from God's purpose; a Pelagian assumption of the innate purity of man; the assertion that the one central factor in all human effort is religion and that religion is founded upon revelation and faith—all these are themes that Herder is constantly expanding and stressing. They are the themes inherent in all his philosophy.

The way to history had been prepared by the method Herder applied in his literary criticism and the *impasse* to which it had led, by Shakespeare, and by the discovery that only religion could provide the means by which he could advance further. Religion now so dominated his mind, that while facilitating his progress, it absorbed history completely. History was thus both the outcome and the servant of religion. Herder studied history so as to know God, rather as he studied Shakespearean drama in order to know Shakespeare. He set himself a dual task, therefore, very much as he had done in his aesthetics. Religion was to explain history and history was to explain religion. As before, this dualism was a source of disharmony.

CHAPTER VI

THE GRADUAL ASCENT

ON the appearance of *Auch Eine Philosophie* in 1774, the *Fragmente*, with other early literary criticism, were finally left behind. Here was a first effort at that historical survey Herder had announced in his *Reisejournal*—an interim survey, to be sure, but at least a practical attempt at the well-nigh impossible. It was the first of a whole series of sketches, as Herder made his way nearer to his central work, the *Ideen*.

If literary criticism had now receded from the foreground, its method and spirit remained. The condemnation of contemporary ineptitude, the laying bare of the true function of things through a study of their origins, and the insistence upon those latent powers that the present neglected—this is common to all Herder's work, whether literary or philosophical. But in his philosophy it was deepened and enriched by the effect of his religious convictions.

Herder stated his purpose in writing this work with no little energy. It was to show how history is the scene of God's activity and how it fulfils His purpose. Herder knew that there is progress behind the course of events—not, as the optimists of the Enlightenment fancied, progress towards happiness and perfection, nor, as the sceptics held, progress without a plan, but progress towards an ultimate goal set by God Himself. The final purpose is veiled and cannot be known till the end, yet each event, each single action or scene in the mighty drama of Providence, is part of the grand progression towards it. The phases in human development grow one out of another. Each is a step towards the final culmination. Man is the blind instrument of fate, an actor in a play of which he cannot know the end; all he can know is that such is his destiny and that he must fulfil it.

That, in Herder's eyes, is the immediate teaching of history. Approached from the proper angle, it is, he knows, an unfailing source of faith and hope and encouragement. He at once appeals for collection and co-ordination of material, so that the central theme of the self-revelation of God and the inevitable marching forward of all things towards His final purpose shall be brought out.

'Hätten wir doch', Herder declares, 'einen solchen Spiegel des Menschengeschlechts in aller Treue, Fülle und Gefühl der Offenbarung Gottes.

Vorarbeiten genug; aber alles in Schlaube und Unordnung! Wir haben unser jetziges Zeitalter fast aller Nationen, und so die Geschichte fast aller Vorzeiten durchkrochen und durchwühlt, ohne fast selbst zu wissen, wozu wir sie durchwühlt haben. Historische Fakta und Untersuchungen, Entdeckungen und Reisebeschreibungen liegen da: wer ist der sie sondere und sichte? . . . Wer, der uns den Tempel Gottes herstelle, wie er in seinem Fortgebäude ist, durch alle Jahrhunderte hindurch! Die ältesten Zeiten der Menschenkindheit sind vorbei: aber Reste und Denkmäler gnug da—die herrlichsten Reste, Unterweisung des Vaters selbst an diese Kindheit—Offenbarung! Sagst du, Mensch, daß sie dir zu alt sei, in deinen zu klugen, altgreisen Jahren—siehe um dich!—der größte Teil von Nationen der Erde ist noch in Kindheit, reden alle noch *die* Sprache, haben *die* Sitten, geben die Vorbilder *des* Grads der Bildung—wohin du unter sogenannte Wilde reisest und horchst, tönen Laute zur Erläuterung der Schrift! wehen lebendige Kommentare der Offenbarung!'[1]

Auch Eine Philosophie is a programme of history. No one realized more than Herder himself that his work was not even a sketch of the survey he had in mind. He begins with human origins. The very first sentence strikes the same note as the *Älteste Urkunde*, without which the work is not fully understandable. He accepts the evidence of the Bible—giving as his main reason for so doing the fact that the philosophers of the Enlightenment did not accept it—and describes the awe and reverence for God, the faith and love, the active cooperation of God and man that marked the beginning of things, asserting that only life lived in this sense corresponds with the intention of Providence. He then turns to the various epochs of human history (or rather of Ancient and European history) to ascertain how far all this had worked out. As he proceeds, Herder's fundamental thesis emerges more and more clearly that mankind is forever changing, always manifesting itself differently, gaining fresh strength, and losing it as well. Like a stream (we are reminded of Goethe's comparison at this point), or a tree, it combines change with

---

[1] V. 565-6; 'If only we had such a mirror of the human race presenting, with complete fidelity, the fullness and awareness of the Revelation of God! Preparations exist in plenty, but everything is, as it were, enclosed in husks, and in confusion. We have crawled and grubbed our way through the present epoch of almost every nation, and similarly the history of almost all past ages, almost without even knowing why. Historical facts and investigations, discoveries and travel-descriptions are at hand. Who is there who will sort them out and sift them? . . . Who is there who will restore the temple of God as the structure it has always been throughout the centuries? The oldest epochs of the childhood of man are gone; but relics and memorials exist in plenty—the most splendid relics of all, the teaching of the Father Himself to the race in its childhood—Revelation! If you say, O Man, that Revelation is too ancient for you, in your all-too-clever senility, look around you. Most of the nations of the earth are still in their childhood, they still speak its language, possess its habits, exhibit its standard of culture, wherever you go among the so-called savage peoples and listen, you hear sounds that illustrate Holy Writ and see the movement of living commentaries upon Revelation.'

continuity, being always one and the same yet always different. Each age, each nation possesses an individuality, with temporal or local characteristics, never to be repeated; it cannot be other than imperfect. It cannot be judged by any standards not its own, since they are equally imperfect; it carries its own criterion within itself.

No one age, therefore, can assume a position of absolute priority. Thus Greece, though idealized, is seen to be no more than a part of the whole ancient world. Conversely, periods that have been neglected are found to have been neglected unjustly, for they too have played their part in human growth as much as any other. Here it is that Herder's most fruitful contribution is made. He discovered in the Middle Ages a time of that faith and naturalness and vigour that were the genuine attributes of humanity in the ideal state. The medieval revival, after the fall of the Ancient world, was the work of the invading Germanic tribes of the North (*ex septentrione lux!*) in collaboration with the civilizing influence of Christianity. With it, new strength and feeling and fertility, alongside a new religion of love and brotherhood and reconciliation, pervaded human civilization. The *gotischer Geist* was one of throbbing vitality and chivalry and piety. All of these things were absent in Herder's own time.

Herder's intention was to show that there was something more in the world besides his own age of reason and Enlightenment. Against this he pours out page after page of the most violent invective. From beneath the burning passion of his attack the eighteenth century emerges as nothing more than a puny phase in human development, no more valuable, indeed a good deal less valuable, than other phases. Thought and abstraction, the twin pillars of the Enlightenment, can never, he declares, bring about real civilization. The plan of Providence shows, on the contrary, that everything evolves from the interaction of organic and environmental causes, and that any other manner of progress is artificial and futile, indeed almost blasphemous. Herder mocks at the inability of his age, in spite of all its learning, to understand that it is different from other ages that came before it, because of different circumstances and not because of the sudden predominance of reason. Such an age, lacking the piety and virility of the great epochs of the past, is bound to be limited, mechanical, and barren. It can, and will, give way to a better future, which must grow out of the small amount of goodness that it contains.

It was an imaginary and poetical vision of the past upon which Herder's conclusions were founded, derived from fiction rather than real data. The effects of his reading of Shakespeare are clearly notice-

E

able in his picture of the Middle Ages. The vitality, colour, chivalry, and romance of those times were certainly taught him by the English dramatist. He saw how these things were the basis upon which the Elizabethan age built, and he felt that this same *romantische Denkart*, the same piety and feeling and strength needed to be recaptured (from the folksong, no doubt) and infused into his own age. The whole of the later achievements of Romantic medieval scholarship in Germany may be derived from this—at first sight somewhat casual—idealization of Herder's and from its more precise repercussions in the *Ideen* and *Humanitätsbriefe*.

The contentions of *Auch Eine Philosophie*, with its many inconsistencies, do not readily group themselves into clear sections of thought. As has been seen, it is an interim production. It is really neither history nor philosophy. Its scope is restricted to antiquity and Western Europe. The reason for this is that Herder intended to give an account of the foundations of contemporary civilization and chose only what was relevant. This competed with his major plan of showing history as the working out of God's purpose; so that it is never quite clear which of these two aims Herder was actually carrying out, or whether or not he was striving to fulfil both at once.

The preoccupation with the present and the future dominates the whole of the last portion of the essay and is undoubtedly responsible for many of its faults. It brings a major element of disunity into the thought of the book, since it contradicts the idea that each age must be valued for its own sake. It quite overwhelms Herder's rival preoccupation with the 'Gang Gottes über die Nationen'.[1] He grows ever more determined to prove his contention that his own age was the outcome of historical causes and not of reason, that it fulfilled the purpose of Providence, not better but worse than some previous ages, that it was no more than a mere link in the chain of progress, not an end in itself but merely a means to an end. We can hear Faust's words to Wagner when Herder exclaims,

'Philosoph, willst du den Stand deines Jahrhunderts ehren und nutzen: das Buch der Vorgeschichte liegt vor dir! mit sieben Siegeln verschlossen; ein Wunderbuch voll Weissagung: auf dich ist das Ende der Tage kommen! lies!'[2]

The whole essay breathes unsuppressed anger at the complacent

[1] V. 565; 'God's movement over all the nations.'
[2] V. 561-2; 'Philosopher, if you desire to honour and to profit the state of your own age, the book of history is before you. It is sealed with seven seals; it is a wonderful book full of prophecy. To you has come the book of the end of all things. Read it.'

acceptance of the Voltairean doctrine of 'wie wirs so herrlich weit gebracht'.[1]

At the same time, however, he saw that, inadequate as it was, his age must form the basis of the future, and when all else in the essay is forgotten the comforting cry is still remembered,

'Laßt uns, meine Brüder, mit mutigem, fröhlichem Herzen auch mitten unter der Wolke arbeiten: denn wir arbeiten zu einer großen Zukunft. Und laßt uns unser Ziel so rein, so hell, so schlackenfrei annehmen, als wirs können: denn wir laufen in Irrlicht und Dämmerung und Nebel.'[2]

Herder, with an eye to at least a perfunctory observance of consistency, discovers elements of good in his own time which must form the foundation of future greatness. His image of the tree that ever renews itself preserves his theme from being utterly impossible, but it is a poetic device that cannot replace the logic that is not there.

The essay reveals a strange mingling of optimism and pessimism. For instance, there is the view that the present is valueless in itself and only exists for the sake of the future, a point which alines Herder with the best in German idealism. Of course, if the emphasis be so apportioned, the future must be regarded as equally valueless! Implicit in this is the willingness, even determination, to sacrifice the present, acknowledged to be of so little value, to a mythical and inscrutable future of possibly corresponding unimportance, in the name of civilization or destiny or Providence. Only the Germans can thus ruthlessly hand over the present. Yet while fatalism dominates the work, the excessive darkening of this fatalism, with the degrading of man to the status of a mere 'ant on the wheel', is most certainly due to Herder's imperious desire to depress the self-importance of contemporary culture. The polemical urge was the enemy of history. He would doubtless have wished the Enlightenment to define itself in the same terms as Mephistopheles, as—

ein Teil von jener Kraft,
Die stets das Böse will und stets das Gute schafft,[3]

or perhaps he would even have preferred to say *gelegentlich* ('occasionally') instead of the second *stets*!

In face of this difficulty, Herder's belief in the continual self-revelation of God in history, which admitted the place of evil as well as

[1] *Faust*, 573; 'What a glorious height we have achieved at last.' (Swanwick's translation.)
[2] V. 580; 'Let us, my brethren, toil with glad, courageous hearts, even though clouded in darkness. For we are toiling towards a great future. And let us take for our goal one that is as pure, as clear, as free from dross as we can; for we walk in delusion, twilight, and mist.'
[3] *Faust*, 1335-6; 'Part of that Power, not understood, which always wills the Bad, and always works the Good.'

good in the scheme of things, saved the situation for him, and brought a measure of hope. Herder found a means that would enable him to eat his cake and have it; he could indulge his anger against the Enlightenment and nevertheless accept it as a preparatory stage of something possibly better. Indeed, without faith in the benevolent wisdom of God, he would have been compelled to regard all human endeavour as futile, and all life as doomed to eternal tragedy. Amid the perplexities and insufficiencies of the world, and in face of man's limited capacities, confidence in the divine guidance of things alone gave consolation. Like Goethe's Iphigenie, Herder to the end of his days clung instinctively and steadfastly to the image of God within his soul. It was an image of his own creation. It is at the centre of all his later philosophy, the philosophy of co-operation with the divine intention through the discovery, development, and exercise of the qualities given by God to man.

No doubt some of the difficulties of *Auch Eine Philosophie* would have been resolved in the second part of the work, which was to have been wholly theological, but which was never written. It was to have expressed this deep religious faith, to have shown that the end of all things was God, just as the *Älteste Urkunde* had shown that the beginning of all things was God. Of this continuation *Maran Atha* and its companion works may be looked upon as preliminary studies. One thing that must have emerged, if the book had been completed, would have been a statement of transcendentalism. This would have placed *Auch Eine Philosophie* in its proper perspective and prevented much needless discussion of its supposed pantheism.

Having produced his manifesto, Herder set himself the task of pointing out how the faults he had exposed might be corrected. A number of works of a limited historical character, planned in part during his journey, now began to appear. He turned first to the field of human psychology. The short prize-essay *Ursachen des gesunkenen Geschmacks* (1775) is a sort of miniature *Auch Eine Philosophie*. It is an *Auch Eine Philosophie* minus its scorching polemic and reduced, pathetically, to form and order. The usual method is followed. Taste is studied in its origins and history. It is declared to be dependent on genius. This latter (significantly described in Faust's words as the 'Ebenbild der Gottheit'[1]) is an embodiment of natural forces, the former being the proportion and balance therein. Without genius, taste cannot exist, while genius on its part is dependent on suitable cultural circumstances. Only in Greece was taste a natural pheno-

---

[1] V. 604; 'The image of God.'

menon, for only there was genius favoured by environment. With the Romans, except in oratory and history, it was an artificial thing, while in modern Europe the cult of imitation, upon which the Renaissance was founded, caused it to grow up with the seeds of its decline within it from the start. If taste is ever to flourish, the conditions for its growth, i.e. for the growth of genius, must be created, and created by education. This was as far as Herder could go in an academic essay in calling for a reconstruction of his age, but the thought was that of his greater work.

Herder was, it will be seen, still working in his favourite field of literature. At the same time, the data he had used for purely critical matters were at hand also for wider purposes. Of the essays that immediately followed, *Vom Erkennen und Empfinden* is quite the most significant, not so much in its published form of 1778 as in its first and second drafts of 1774 and 1775. The substance of this work is simple enough. It is that feeling and experience are the basis and origin of all thought. The soul knows only what is given to it by experience, which Herder calls 'the finger of God'; it knows nothing from within itself. While thought thus depends upon feeling, feeling depends very little upon thought. Herder is not slow to point out the corollary of this—

'folge der Natur! sei kein Polyp ohne Kopf und keine Steinbüste ohne Herz; laß den Strom deines Lebens frisch in deiner Brust schlagen, aber auch zum feinen Mark deines Verstandes hinauf geläutert, und da Lebensgeist werden.'[1]

It is the harmonious interaction of thought and feeling that must be achieved above all; thought must guide the effects of feeling.

'Wo sollte es in deine Vernunft kommen, wenn nicht durch Empfindung? würde der Kopf denken, wenn dein Herz nicht schlüge? Aber gegenteils, willst du auf jedes Pochen und Wallen deines Herzens, auf jeden Nachhall einer gereizten Fiber, als auf die Stimme Gottes merken, und ihr blindlings folgen, wo kannst du hingeraten? da alsdenn dein Verstand zu spät kommt.'[2]

Out of such perfect co-ordination will emerge something approximating to Spinoza's intellectual love of God.

The earlier drafts of the work are less positive but more dynamic.

[1] VIII. 201; 'Follow nature. Do not be a polyp without a head or a stone statue without a heart. Let the current of life beat freshly in your heart, but also, being purified, serve to strengthen your understanding; thus it will become the spirit of life.'

[2] VIII. 201; 'Whence would anything come to your reason, if not through feeling? Would the head think, if the heart did not beat? On the other hand, if you are to heed every beat and surge of your heart, every message of a stimulated nerve, as if it were the voice of God, and follow it blindly, where will you be? If you do, your reason will act too late.'

No one human sense, declares Herder, can apprehend the whole
universe, therefore the Creator gave us several so that we may apprehend various aspects of it. The soul is attached to the universe through
the body, which is a symbol of the universe; it apprehends through
the body, i.e. the feelings. Everything it apprehends is symbolical
of ultimate truth and perfection; symbolical since most of the universe
is unknown to us who have not the requisite means wherewith to
apprehend it. Indeed, all beings that are limited, i.e. all beings but
God, can grasp only a part of the universe. We feel little, but in that
little much is symbolized.

'Ein Mensch, der stark in sich selbst ist, fühlt sich in alles tief hinein;
empfindet weniges, aber das wenige viel. Er hat nur *seine* Situationen, wo
er ist, da ist er aber auch innig. . . . Ein Mensch, der sich durch alle Glieder,
Sehnen und Muskeln also ganz und wohl fühlt, ein in starker Wahrheit
alles empfangende Mensch: welch ein Ebenbild der Stärke des Schöpfers !'[1]

With this clear parallel of the *Urfaust* in mind, we are no longer
surprised to discover that reason is described in terms that are verbally
akin to Goethe's. 'Dieser Strahl der Gottheit'[2] is a quality that is given
to human beings alone; it raises them above the animals; with its aid
they are empowered to construct their image of God and the universe.
In a significantly Faustian paragraph Herder sums up:

'Das ist also das Hauptgesetz, wonach die Natur beide Kräfte geordnet:
nämlich, daß Empfindung wirke, wo noch kein Erkennen sein kann: daß
diese Vieles auf Einmal dunkel in die Seele bringe, damit diese es sich bis
zu Einem Grad aufkläre und ein Resultat ihres Wesens darin finde: daß
dies auf die leichteste angenehmste Art geschehe, damit das Meistmögliche
in der kürzesten Zeit erkannt und die Seele sanft fortgeführt im Wirken
außer sich werde, als ob sie allein mit sich wirkte und sich beschäftigte.
Großes Meisterstück der mütterlichen Vorsehung, und ihm bleibt die
Seele bei jedem Schritte des Daseins, selbst in Nebel und Irrtum, treu.—
("Ein guter Mensch in seinem dunklen Drange. . . .") Es entwickelt sich
aus den gegebnen Grundsätzen eine Philosophie der Seele, des Weltalls, der
Gottheit, über die ich mir nichts Erhebenderes denke. In jedem kleinsten
Teile des Unendlichen herrscht die Wahrheit, Weisheit, Güte des Ganzen:
in jedem Erkenntnis, wie in jeder Empfindung spiegelt sich das Bild Gottes,
dort mit Strahlen oder Schimmer des reinen Lichts, hier mit Farben, in die
sich der Sonnenstrahl teilte. Erkennen ist Glanz der Sonne genießen, die

---

[1] VIII. 309; 'A man who is strong within himself projects his feelings into everything. He
will not feel much, but that little he will feel powerfully. There exist for him only the situations
in which he finds himself, but he is in them with all his heart. A man who thus feels completely
in every one of his limbs, senses, muscles, a really all-receptive man, what an image he is of the
power of the Creator !'
[2] VIII. 299; 'This light from God.'

sich in jedem Strahle abspiegelt: Empfindung ist ein Farbenspiel des Regenbogens, schön, wahr, aber nur als Abglanz der Sonne. ("Am farbigen Abglanz haben wir das Leben.") Geht diese klar auf am Firmamente, so verschwindet der Regenbogen mit all seinen Farben.'[1]

These sentences point the way to the *Ideen* more clearly than ever, and *Vom Erkennen und Empfinden* occupies a major position in the progress towards this work. The mission Herder has set before himself is the all-embracing study of human psychology and history. This involves the primary task of discovering what it is that is the special endowment of man. He regards this as the most urgent and elevating task there is or can be. His slogan is: 'Verehre also den Genius deines Geschlechts und suche, so rein du kannst, ihm zu dienen'.[2]

Both the positive and the negative aspects of the *Sturm und Drang* are contained within this work. On the one hand, there is set out the despair of the movement, arising from the utter impossibility of knowing anything more than what must be regarded as a symbol. On the other hand, there is the teaching that man is created in a special way for this world, that he may know what he is intended to know (but no more), and that within his limitations his powers must be cultivated to the full. Here are the two sides of the medal, just as there are two sides to Faust, who denies and despairs, and yet affirms and strives. None of Herder's writings, indeed, is so completely Faustian as this one, which declares *Erkennen* and *Empfinden* to be the attributes of the two souls in man's breast.[3]

The way to the *Ideen* was, however, long and tedious. Meantime, other works carried Herder's thought further. The *Plastik*, a contemporary production of *Vom Erkennen und Empfinden*, analyses human

---

[1] VIII. 246; 'This is therefore the principal law according to which nature has regulated both faculties; namely, that feeling operates where perception cannot yet be; that it introduces a great deal at once into the soul obscurely, so that this latter may clarify it to some extent and discover thereby what its own existence can achieve; that this takes place in the easiest and pleasantest possible way, so that the greatest possible amount may be perceived in the shortest possible time, and the soul may be gently led forth outside itself in its operations, as if it were operating in isolation and concerned only with itself. A great masterpiece of the motherly work of Providence, and to it the soul remains true at every step in its existence, even in darkness and error. (A good man, through obscurest aspiration, has still an instinct of the one true way.— *Faust*, 328-9.) There develops from the given premisses a philosophy of the soul, of the universe, of God, and I can imagine nothing more elevating than that. In every minute part of the infinite prevails the truth, wisdom and goodness of the whole; in every perception, as in every feeling, is reflected the image of God, there with the rays or the brilliance of white light, here in colours into which the sunbeam is divided. Perception is to enjoy the splendour of the sun, which is reflected in its every beam; feeling is the opalescence of the rainbow, beautiful, real, but only a reflection of the sun. (*Faust*, 4727. Life is not light, but the refracted colour.) If the latter rises clearly in the firmament, the rainbow with all its colours disappears.'

[2] VIII. 301; 'Honour, therefore, the genius of mankind and seek to serve it as purely as you can.'

[3] VIII. 307.

feeling in even greater detail in its particular relation to the plastic arts. This work, likewise, must be read as an apotheosis of feeling in the *Sturm und Drang* sense. It defines Herder's aesthetic position in its relation to his expanding outlook. It marks an advance upon Lessing's distinctions between the arts and sets them on a different footing by deriving painting from the visual sense and sculpture from the sense of touch, the former being the more intellectual, the latter the more emotional of the two. Aesthetic appreciation is shown to rest upon a sympathetic interpretation on the part of the spectator, and is simultaneously revealed as a channel through which the whole of humanity may be known. Herder traces artistic creation back to the mental and emotional processes that were at work in the artist, very much as he had dealt with poetic production in the *Fragmente*. He praises the human form as an image of the divine, and studies its features as manifestations of the soul. Beauty is declared to be the expression of inner perfection in its creator. Appreciation of beauty is similarly a re-living of that inner perfection on the part of the observer, by means of a complete transference of himself into the object he observes. Not only is the sense of touch intimately concerned in this process, but the entire soul of the spectator is involved and must be suitably attuned.

The historical trend emerges clearly in the three prize-essays of these years concerning the relationship of literature to life. They may all of them be regarded as commentaries upon the *Volkslieder*, defining more closely than the prefaces to that work the real intention that was in Herder's mind. *Über die Wirkung der Dichtkunst* is the most significant and in many ways the most attractive of the three. It shares with the others a more markedly systematic outline than has hitherto been apparent in any of Herder's writings. Its aim is to show the influence of literature upon civilization—the method being thus the direct opposite of that of the *Fragmente*. Literary criticism is now placed completely in the service of historiography. Yet the material is substantially the same; it is the point of view, the allocation of emphasis, the presentation that is different. The essence of poetry is still regarded as 'energy', its effect still ascribed to its being the channel through which feeling is transmitted. The poet is seen in the light of a spokesman of God, a prophet, priest, and lawgiver, and poetry proclaimed as the most powerful human educating force. The findings of the Shakespeare-essay concerning the qualities of original genius are developed almost to the stage reached in Schiller's *Briefe über die ästhetische Erziehung des Menschen*, except that Herder gives to the ethical the priority over the aesthetic. For not all poetry can have a good effect—even in Greece he discovers artificiality and childishness that give pleasure without giving betterment, and, remarkably foreshadowing modern Aristotelian interpretation, he asserts that the whole idea of the cathartic effect of tragedy was merely an ingenious excuse for art that lacked the great primitive educative qualities.

Herder proceeds to give a complete survey of the history of literature from Classical to modern times. Once again he derives much instruction from the Middle Ages. The poetry of the northern (including Celtic) nations, he points out, materially assisted these nations in changing the whole face of Europe, since it kept the national soul alive. The Wonderful in medieval poetry was in its turn provided by the Arabs; this, fused with the contribution of northern nations and of Christianity, gave the world the literature and culture of chivalry. Herder has words of commendation for the *Minnesang*, the Arthurian epic, and the religious poetry of Dante and Langland. The coming of the Renaissance, in his opinion, killed the vital effect of poetry, which became a fine art, a thing of scholarship, without spontaneity and immediacy. Foreshadowing Schlegel, Herder puts in a word for the novel as being capable of giving a complete and positively influential picture of an age, and concludes with a bitter indictment of his own country for neglecting its past treasures and producing literature only for scholars and reviewers.

The essay is really a history of culture as well as a history of poetry, conceived mainly in the spirit of *Auch Eine Philosophie*. It is filled out and developed by the two companion essays, which at the same time move considerably nearer to the *Ideen*. Indeed, the final transition seems to have been achieved in this period 1778-80. *Über den Einfluß der schönen in die höheren Wissenschaften* answers an old problem of Herder's in declaring that the arts and sciences are impossible without a well-balanced life as a pre-requisite, so that a reform of life must precede a reform of letters.

'Die höchste Wissenschaft ist ohne Zweifel die Kunst zu leben; und wie manchen haben seine schönen Wissenschaften um diese Einzige, diese göttliche Kunst gebracht!'[1]

he writes in terms that continue his long-standing condemnation of modern times. Again anticipating Schiller, he asks for a perfect balance between heart and head. The senses are infallible, but their

[1] IX. 294; 'The highest knowledge is undoubtedly the art of living; and how many men have been robbed by their fine arts of this one thing, this divine art.'

operations must nevertheless be guided and harmonized by reason. The arts must assist by developing and bringing order into our emotions and fancies, and by teaching 'humanity'.

'Die schönen Wissenschaften sind also, oder sollen sein Ordnerinnen der Sinne, der Einbildungskraft, der Neigungen und Begierden: das Sehglas also zur Wahrheit, die sich uns Sterblichen immer nur im Schein offenbart, die Arbeiterinnen, den Grund unsrer Seelen zu ordnen, damit Wahrheit und Tugend sich ihnen offenbare.'[1]

A training in literature and art is, therefore, an essential preparation for higher studies, based upon reason, since otherwise the emotional side of man's nature would be neglected. Art therefore has a definite educational purpose and must be conscious of it.

The third of the prize-essays, *Vom Einfluß der Regierung auf die Wissenschaften und der Wissenschaften auf die Regierung*, approaches a stage nearer to the goal. It gives yet another history of culture, after the manner of *Über die Wirkung der Dichtkunst*, with the emphasis slightly changed. Such general surveys are by now becoming a habit with Herder.

His purpose is to explain why the arts and sciences have not flourished at all times and in all places, and he finds the answer to this in political conditions. He therefore discusses various forms of government, belonging to various nations, in their relationship to the arts. It is not always clear whether Herder is characterizing political systems or literatures, so closely does his work approximate to a general history of human civilization. Greek republicanism is praised as being responsible for fostering spontaneity, measure, and humanity in the arts, but the Middle Ages are now roundly condemned as a period of superstition, darkness, and confusion; there is none of the enthusiasm that was contained in *Auch Eine Philosophie*. The general conclusion is reached that the more a government is animated by wisdom and humanity, the better the arts will flourish. Herder re-echoes that eulogy of freedom of thought in a republican state that Schiller's *Don Carlos* expressed a year or two earlier, but modifies his results by claiming that a censorship should be imposed upon art that is frivolous or hinders human happiness and welfare. He admits the state's right to exercise compulsion upon its members for their own good. Art is, thus, clearly subordinated to morality, and its power to mould the entire character of a people is once again stressed.

[1] IX. 296; 'The fine arts, thus, are, or should be, regulators of our senses, our fancy, our inclinations and desires; the lens to show us truth, which is revealed to us mortals only as a reflection; the artisans who regulate the whole foundations of our souls, so that truth and goodness may be revealed to them.'

It is really to this phase in Herder's authorship that his *Volkslieder* belong. They provide the practical example in support of his general theories. If his unpublished collection of 1774 had been primarily literary in its purpose, the second anthology was first and foremost a contribution to the study of general human history. For this reason Herder was no longer terrified into withdrawal by the boorishness of Nicolai. The latter, behindhand as usual, had only just been in time to grasp the literary intention of the earlier folksong collection, an intention that was now superseded. The basic fact is as clear as ever, that poetry is the axis on which all Herder's thought turned. It never recedes into the background, even for a fleeting moment. The ever-present stand-by, it is always there to afford example and infallible instruction; it is for Herder at all times the most reliable guide to the complexities of the history of man and of his self-expression.

There only remains to be noted a parallel metamorphosis that took place in Herder's theological writings during these remarkable years; for the religious basis on which *Auch Eine Philosophie* rested, provided equally, when clarified and balanced, the foundation for the *Ideen*. The *Provinzialblätter*, with aggressive impetuosity, had asserted that the most powerful transmission of the Word of God was by a direct appeal to feeling and faith, without any contaminating interference at the hands of reason. As Faust said:

Wenn ihr's nicht fühlt, ihr werdet's nicht erjagen.[1]

Or in Herder's words:

'Die ganze Religion in Grund und Wesen ist Tatsache! Geschichte! Auf Zeugnis der Sinne und nicht der Oberkräfte allein; bei dem Empfangenden auf Glauben, der alle Kräfte faßt, gebaut: nach Zweck und Inhalt ans Volk, den größten sinnlichern Teil der Menschheit, und nicht an Grübler gerichtet; in Art und Sprache sie mit allen Trieben umzuschaffen und zu lenken. So predigten die Apostel Jesum und philosophierten nicht: so redeten die Propheten als Stimmen Gottes! Glaube aus der Predigt, die Herz und Sinne und den ganzen Menschen traf.'[2]

[1] *Faust*, 534; 'You'll ne'er attain it, save you know the feeling.'
[2] VII. 265; 'The whole of religion is basically and essentially a thing of fact, of history. It rests upon the testimony of the senses and not of the higher faculties alone; in the person who receives it, it rests on faith which lays hold of all the faculties. It is directed, in its purpose and content, to the people, to the greatest and the more emotional part of mankind, and not to over-subtle reasoners; so as to transform and guide them, together with all their impulses, in manner and language. Thus the Apostles preached Jesus Christ; they did not philosophize; thus the prophets spoke, as the mouthpiece of God. Faith emerged from their preaching, which touched the heart, the senses, the whole of man's being.'

So runs a very significant passage. It is an easy transition from this, on the one hand, to the demand for a study of the human soul that receives religion, and, on the other hand, to a more general fusion of religion and history. The belief that the Bible should be studied historically if its truth is to be grasped, leads to the conviction that all history can shed light upon its teaching. The plant is to be known by a study of the seed and the seed by a study of the plant. Only, in the outcome, the study of the plant possesses so many ramifications that it ultimately dwarfs all else, though the seed is never lost sight of by the conscientious investigator.

The *Theologische Briefe*, with the illustration of their requirements in *Vom Geist der Ebräischen Poesie*, supplement the *Provinzialblätter*. From his opening contention that the Bible, like all other literature, should be studied 'humanly' and genetically, in the spirit in which it was written, Herder proceeds to some telling pronouncements upon the interrelation of nature and Revelation which are fundamental to his historical position. History is contemplated in the most comprehensive sense possible, so that everything is seen to be a branch of history. Nature and Revelation are gifts of God and mutually explanatory. God shows us His works and teaches us how to understand them and so to recognize Him and His purpose. *We* see things only from a very narrow angle and for a brief moment of time. *He* is infinite, *we* are finite. He instructs us, helps us to make use of our faculties in order that we may see the fullness and harmony of things and their relationship to ourselves. This instruction is always in progress; history is its story and the earth its theatre. We are pilgrims in this world, preparing for the eternal fatherland to come.

The Bible was the starting point of the *Ideen* just as much as it was of *Auch Eine Philosophie*. It provided the basic sense of unity and continuity in all things; it presented the most complete and perfect ideal of human life; it gave the key to the world's mystery. The world, in turn, afforded the commentary upon the Bible's teaching. The way was clear for the comprehensive survey to be written. The Bible-studies themselves provided an important section of the coming work ready-made, in that *Vom Geist der Ebräischen Poesie* evolved a cultural survey of early Jewish history. Nothing now remained but to compose similar surveys of other peoples and to co-ordinate them into the general scheme. The real harvest of the genetical method of the *Fragmente* was about to be reaped.

CHAPTER VII

THE PHILOSOPHY OF HISTORY

AFTER completing these miniatures, Herder was ready to tackle his full-scale plan. The structure was clear, the detail needed to be filled in. Hitherto he had drawn sketch-maps on special projections to bring out certain factors. Now he had to include the whole earth, in all its fullness, on one projection only. He had to fit in new countries and continents, with their physical, political, historical, meteorological, and biological features. As he worked, he made many discoveries. He read prodigiously. He owed much to the encouragement of friends, to Knebel, to Einsiedel, and above all to Goethe. With the latter he lived daily in the closest touch, at a time when Goethe was himself immersed in his study of morphology—indeed his discovery of the intermaxillary bone in man came just after the completion of Herder's first volume of the *Ideen*. The debt of Strassburg was handsomely repaid by pupil to master in these years of delightful mutual illumination. Yet all the time Herder was disquieted and dissatisfied. He had thrust aside the *Ebräische Poesie*, unfinished; he wrestled with church accounts; he felt keenly, especially in the later stages of the *Ideen*, that he really could not freely speak his mind, particularly on politics and religion; and he was embittered by the severity of Kant's criticism of the first parts of his work. Thus the peak of Herder's achievement remained a fragment, like everything else. The 'bits left over' became fragments of other fragmentary works.

The *Ideen*, Suphan declared, are to Herder as *Faust* is to Goethe, the apex to which all else led the way. The ideas of historical continuity, of nationality, and of the value of literature as the key to the understanding of the human soul, had busied him from the start. Then theology had assumed priority. It still dominated Herder's history, though his standpoint was now considerably more secularized. The *Ideen* supplemented *Auch Eine Philosophie* (of which they were to have been the second edition), with scientific data and philosophical reflections, and gave completeness to what Herder had himself pronounced to be a 'fliegendes Blatt', a pamphlet. The same *idée maîtresse* was there as before—to study history as revealing 'der Gang Gottes in der Natur, die Gedanken, die der Ewige uns in der Reihe seiner Werke tätlich dargelegt hat,'[1]—to explain it, therefore, as the teacher of the truths of religion. Herder applied himself to history, just as Ranke confesses *he* did, as the approach to God, believing that the destiny of man can only be read out of the book of all Creation.

The work opens in a manner that turns our thoughts at once to the 'Prologue in Heaven' in *Faust*. The archangels' song, with its praise of the omniscience of God, the serene causality within all nature, and the restless change and activity on the earth, is a sort of small-scale *Ideen*. 'Vom Himmel muß unsere Philosophie der Geschichte des menschlichen Geschlechts anfangen.'[2] Man's destiny is governed by those same eternal laws by which the whole universe is governed. The world is itself a star among other stars. It affords, thanks to its position in relation to the sun, its rotation and the inclination of its axis, circumstances that favour human life. Its plant and animal systems are stages in the rising scale of being that culminates in man.

Herder, therefore, demands that greater attention be paid to the importance of geography, botany, and zoology. He himself applies the comparative method, so as to discover man's special distinguishing feature, and finds this to be his upright posture. From this, and the consequent vertical carriage of the head, everything specifically human may be accounted for. It is that which gives man the brain which he needs for the growth of his reasoning power, and at the same time, it is symbolical of his 'uprightness', his upward striving. Man is constituted—'organized' is Herder's word—to speak, to reason, to develop and use 'higher faculties'. Such is the law of nature, declares Herder, managing to combine the determinism inherent in his view of the universe with the concept of free will that is fundamental in his view of man. Man comes upon the earth to learn to reason. Indeed, he must learn all things; the ability to learn is his special gift, and he must use it. Even though he errs he will finally reach truth through error. He does not bring reason with him. It is something to be acquired, something which no beast possesses, but which belongs to man alone. It is the result of accumulated experience, and the primary aid in developing it is speech.

'Vernunft ist nichts als etwas Vernommenes, eine gelernte Proportion und Richtung der Ideen und Kräfte, zu welcher der Mensch nach seiner Organisation und Lebensweise gebildet worden. Eine Vernunft der Engel kennen wir nicht: so wenig als wir den innern Zustand eines tiefern

---

[1] XIII. 9; 'The progress of God in nature, the intentions which the Eternal has presented to us in the actuality of all His works.'

[2] XIII. 13; 'Our philosophy of the history of the human race must begin in heaven.'

Geschöpfs unter uns innig einsehen; die Vernunft des Menschen ist menschlich.'[1]

By virtue of his reasoning power man is of the world and yet above it—'more than a cherub,' as Faust says of himself. He has two souls within him. He alone is free. He alone can choose,

> Er unterscheidet,
> Wählet und richtet,[2]

where all other creatures are bound by instinct. He alone strives to discover and follow the ways of God in nature.

'Alle seine Versuche hierüber, selbst wo er irrte oder nur träumen konnte, sind Beweise seiner Majestät, einer gottähnlichen Kraft und Hoheit. Das Wesen, das alles schuf, hat wirklich einen Strahl seines Lichts, einen Abdruck der ihm eigensten Kräfte in unsre schwache Erdorganisation gelegt,'[3]

writes Herder in a manner that foreshadows the thought and even the very words of the 'Prologue in Heaven'. The whole Faustian scheme is everywhere present—the presiding wisdom of God, the eternal striving, the two souls, the 'Schein des Himmelslichts',[4] the pursuit of truth through error; and it belongs to a period when Herder was in the closest contact with the—supposedly—non-Faustian Goethe, the Goethe of early Weimar Classicism. Before long we shall come upon the Mephistophelian element too!

Reason enables man to achieve what the rest of nature can not. It gives him the power to adapt himself to climatic variations; it renders it possible for him to develop finer impulses and senses, an artistic ability, peacefulness, sociability, freedom, lawfulness, and, above all, the ideas of religion and immortality. All these are comprised in the compendious term *Humanität*.

'Ich wünschte, daß ich in das Wort Humanität alles fassen könnte, was ich bisher über des Menschen edle Bildung zur Vernunft und Freiheit, zu feinern Sinnen und Trieben, zur zartesten und stärksten Gesundheit, zur Erfüllung und Beherrschung der Erde gesagt habe: denn der Mensch hat

---

[1] XIII. 145; 'Reason is nothing else but what is perceived, an acquired proportion and direction in the ideas and faculties for which man has been constructed, both in his constitution and in his manner of life. We do not know of reason belonging to the angels, any more than we can understand the mental state of any creature lower than ourselves. The reason of man is human.'

[2] Goethe, 'Das Göttliche'; 'He can discriminate, choose, and judge.'

[3] XIII. 148; 'All his attempts concerning this, even when he has erred or could do no more than vainly dream, are proofs of his sovereignty, a godlike power and nobility. The Being who created all things has indeed placed in our weak earthly vessel a ray of His light and the mark of His own particular faculties.'

[4] *Faust*, 284; 'The gleam of heavenly light.'

kein edleres Wort für seine Bestimmung als Er selbst ist, in dem das Bild
des Schöpfers unsrer Erde, wie es hier sichtbar werden konnte, abgedruckt
lebt.'[1]

There are other and fuller definitions than this one, but the fundamental factor is brought out at every stage, that *Humanität* is something of which man alone is capable, and which he must learn to
develop for himself in this life. The supreme aim of human philosophy is to discover and define *Humanität* and to point the way to
its achievement.

Its highest quality is religion, the sphere in which man's higher
nature is most fully developed. Like reason, religion has a natural
origin—in the search for causality, for the prime source of things,
God. This is something that cannot be perceived, only surmised and
believed. Herder moves very near to Kant's unknowable *Ding an
sich* here, just as he approaches Kant's idea of duty when he declares
that man must submit himself willingly to the laws of nature.

At this point Herder turns to his favourite theme of immortality.
In 1781, his 'Gespräche über die Seelenwanderung' had objected to the
view of metempsychosis (which he himself had once held), put forward by Schlosser, and by Lessing in the *Erziehung des Menschengeschlechts*. Transmigration was not enough for Herder. It was the
opposite of that progressive development, that endless striving after
higher spheres that is fundamental to his philosophy. The soul, the
peak of all being, must go on with its endeavours even though the
body may perish. There is no death, only change, transition to a
higher life. This world is a place of preparation. For, unless the
Creator was in error when He constructed us for the purpose of
Humanität, which cannot be realized perfectly in this imperfect life,
the goal must be something that transcends it all. The process, like
that of Romantic thought, is a progressive one. In his weakness and
confusion, man must win his way gradually to the light. The striving
after *Humanität* continues in the next world. We leave our earthly
limitations behind us; they have served their purpose by causing us to
strive after more perfect things.

'Es ist befremdend und doch unleugbar, daß unter allen Erdbewohnern
das menschliche Geschlecht dem Ziel seiner Bestimmung am meisten fern
bleibt. Jedes Tier erreicht, was es in seiner Organisation erreichen soll; der

---

[1] XIII. 154; 'I wish that I could include in this word *Humanität* everything that I have said
so far about the noble constitution of man for reason and freedom, finer senses and impulses,
the most delicate and most robust health, the realization of the purpose of the world and
rulership over it. For man has no nobler word for his destiny than himself, in whom the image
of the Creator of our earth lives in that form which could here be made manifest.'

einzige Mensch erreichts nicht, eben weil sein Ziel so hoch, so weit, so unendlich ist und er auf unserer Erde so tief, so spät, mit so viel Hindernissen von außen und innen anfängt. Dem Tier ist die Muttergabe der Natur, sein Instinkt, der sichere Führer; es ist noch als Knecht im Hause des obersten Vaters und muß gehorchen. Der Mensch ist schon als Kind in demselben und soll, außer einigen notdürftigen Trieben, alles was zur Vernunft und Humanität gehört, erst lernen. Er lernts also unvollkommen, weil er mit dem Samen des Verstandes und der Tugend auch Vorurteile und üble Sitten erbt und in seinem Gange zur Wahrheit und Seelenfreiheit mit Ketten beschwert ist, die vom Anfange seines Geschlechts herreichen.'[1]

'Wahrheit, Schönheit und Liebe waren das Ziel, nach dem der Mensch in jeder seiner Bemühungen, auch ihm selbst unbewußt und oft auf so unrechten Wegen strebte; das Labyrinth wird sich entwirren, die verführenden Zaubergestalten werden schwinden und ein jeder wird, fern oder nahe, nicht nur den Mittelpunkt sehn, zu dem sein Weg geht, sondern Du wirst ihn auch, mütterliche Vorsehung, unter der Gestalt des Genius und Freundes deß er bedarf, mit verzeihender sanfter Hand selbst zu ihm leiten.'[2]

The *Ideen*, then, provide a perfect commentary to the concluding teachings of *Faust*, as they do to the opening scenes; Faust's confusion, blindness, and error, his 'dunkler Drang', his tireless effort, the deceptive allurements of ease and pleasure and the passing beauty of the moment, the purification, the final blaze of understanding, the intercession by Gretchen, the *Liebe von oben* and the endless *Hinanziehen*—all these are amply covered by Herder's contentions.

The parallel grows ever closer and more instructive. Man belongs to two worlds. As an earthly being he can be satisfied with earthly things, as a heavenly being he sees only imperfection around him. Thus, man alone is in conflict with the world and himself, and complete happiness and complete self-realization in this earthly life are

[1] XIII. 190; 'It is strange but undeniable that among all inhabitants of the earth the human race remains furthest from the goal of its destiny. Every beast attains to what its constitution intends it to attain. Man alone does not do so, because his goal is so high, so ample, so infinite, and he begins upon our earth so humbly, so late, and with so many obstacles within and outside him. The sure guide of the animal is his instinct, the gift of Mother Nature. The animal is still a slave in the house of the Father on high, and must obey. Man is in this house as a child, and apart from some necessary impulses, has to learn everything that appertains to reason and humanity. Thus he learns imperfectly, because he inherits, not only the germ of reason and virtue, but also prejudices and bad habits, and is hampered on his way to truth and spiritual freedom by chains that come down from the beginnings of the race.'
[2] XIII. 191-2; 'Truth, beauty, and love have always been the goal after which man has striven, in every one of his endeavours, even when he was not conscious of it and strove in very erroneous ways. The labyrinth will cease to be confusing, the seductive shapes of unreality will pass away, and not only will every one, from near or far, see the central point to which his way leads, but thou, Mother Providence, wilt guide him thyself with gentle, forgiving hands, in the guise of the guardian angel and friend whom he needs.'

F

impossible. So life is a struggle—unless man be indolent—and the reward is the hereafter. 'Trägheit ist die Erbsünde der Menschen.'[1] To strive and to do—in that alone can personality be developed and preserved and an after-life achieved. In that alone can the soul assert its permanence. The unhappy fate that befalls the inactive hand-maidens at the end of the 'Helena tragedy' in *Faust*, namely the loss of their identities and their fading into nature to start on entirely different existences, that too is inherent in Herder's view. Read side by side, the fifth book of the *Ideen* and the second part of *Faust* shed much light one upon the other. Can we ever doubt the debt that Goethe owed to his master, not merely in the formation of his philosophy but in its final evolution? The thought-progression is in both these major works that of poetry not of logic; and Kant's condemnations on the latter score should no more affect our appreciation of the whole of the *Ideen* than rationalist criticism of the conclusion of *Faust* should impair our enjoyment of the poem. The thought *is* coherent, and *is* understandable. The unity is an artistic one. The approach is that of the imaginative preacher rather than of the objective scientist.

The first volume of the *Ideen* is best regarded as an entity in itself. It reached a height that was never afterwards accessible to Herder. The second volume opens on a brilliant level, but ends in a most unconvincing manner. For one thing, Herder was disturbed by the icy hostility of Kant, and he allowed his resentment to deflect him from his real course into the field of polemical writing. Hence he consciously, and inconsistently, proceeded to stress the ideal of happiness as the aim of humanity, and further, simply in order to set himself up against his critic's political views, reverted to the Rousseauism he had once despised. So that Kant's review of this volume is indeed justified. It lacks clarity; it is contradictory and unsatisfying. Even before he had really started to draw his map, Herder was adopting quite a different projection from that with which he had begun.

In this second part Herder studies the divisions of mankind, and the many individual variations displayed. The idea of nationality, with its sources in geographical environment and hereditary distinctions, is brought out as the leading factor in history. Nature, he sees, has not favoured each nation equally, though she compensates for defects in other ways. All in their turn rise and flourish and decline, as eternal Creation continues its perpetual process of self-renewal.

If there is much here that alines Herder with Hegel and with Speng-

---

[1] XIV. 567; 'Indolence is the original sin of mankind.'

ler, there is also a good deal in what he says concerning human origins to suggest that he was a precursor of Darwin. But science had still much ground to cover before it reached the doctrine of evolution. Herder believed firmly in the idea that man is a special creation, and he held to the view of the original oneness of the human race. He did not at all depart from orthodoxy in this matter. The theologian and poet in him were stronger than the man of science. At all points his sense of wonder and his adoration for the wisdom of nature dominated his work; and when he saw what he considered to be a deviation from nature's wise intentions, his bitterness was all the sharper. He condemned the shortcomings of his own time as angrily now as he had done in the Bückeburg years. He rebelled against the obsession with knowledge and speculation and preached the doctrine of practical activity in as forthright terms as Faust himself. Our lives are given to us to use, he declared, or they will decay. Our personalities must achieve permanence through useful and healthy activity; that is the first rule of happiness. This is the complete answer to *Weltschmerz*—the *Weltschmerz* that he himself knew only too well.

'Unsern vielorganischen Körper mit allen seinen Sinnen und Gliedern empfingen wir zum Gebrauch, zur Übung. Ohne diese stocken unsre Lebenssäfte; unsere Organe werden matt; der Körper, ein lebendiger Leichnam, stirbt lange vorher ehe er stirbt; er verweset eines langsamen, elenden, unnatürlichen Todes. . . . Ein mit Kenntnissen überfüllter Kopf und wenn es auch goldene Kenntnisse wären; er erdrückt den Leib, verengt die Brust, verdunkelt den Blick und wird dem, der ihn trägt, eine kranke Last des Lebens. . . . Nur auf dem Gebrauch der ganzen Seele, insonderheit ihrer tätigen Kräfte, ruht der Segen der Gesundheit; und da laßt uns abermals der Vorsehung danken, daß sie es mit dem Ganzen des Menschengeschlechts nicht zu fein nahm und unsre Erde zu nichts weniger als einem Hörsaal gelehrter Wissenschaften bestimmte.'[1]

Thus, only in purposeful, positive activity can man achieve happiness in himself and in his existence and, like Faust, say to the moment as it passes, while duly regarding it as no more than a symbol of the eternal, 'Tarry awhile, thou art so fair!' The guidance as to how man

[1] XIII. 334-6; 'We were given our bodies, which are constituted for so many things, along with all their senses and members, for use, for employment. Otherwise our vital humours stagnate; our organs become slack. The body, like a living corpse, dies long before its time; it decays in a slow, miserable, unnatural death. . . . A head too full of knowledge, even though such knowledge be golden, stifles the body, constricts the chest, darkens the sight and becomes an unhealthy burden to the life of its possessor. . . . The blessing of health is founded only on the use of all our soul, particularly of its active faculties; and here let us thank Providence once again for not having made too delicate a job of all the human race and for not having intended our earth to be a lecture-room for learned studies.'

must act, is given, now as in the *Sturm und Drang* period, by the heart
not the head, the feelings not the intellect.

But for one thing, indeed, we might almost imagine ourselves for
a moment back in the world of Strassburg and Bückeburg—and this
is the doctrine of measure, the balanced co-ordination of our strength
and direction of our effort. We must strive, if we are to fulfil ourselves,
but our striving must be properly governed. Our lives must be
symmetrically ordered. Self-cultivation involves self-restraint; not
only the development of our powers but also, where necessary,
the renunciation of superfluity. This ideal is a further outcome of the
vision of creative personality which had appealed to Herder in the
Sturm und Drang years, only now unbounded irrationalism has grown
into the maturer conception of serene self-discipline. The apotheosis
of passion has yielded to the acknowledgement of the reconciling
function of reason, for reason itself is part of nature's machinery, no
longer the enemy but the guide of the senses and emotions.

All this leads to Herder's restatement of the Greek ideal of measure,
presided over by the rehabilitated figure of Nemesis. Any violation
of the principles of humanity or betrayal of the powers entrusted to
man will unavoidably bring down retribution upon itself. Lack of
balance will automatically carry with it the germs of its own destruction. The universe is governed by an inherent legality, and effect
follows upon cause with mathematical inevitability.

'Zu einer ins Unermeßliche wachsenden Fülle der Gedanken und der
Empfindungen ist weder unser Haupt noch unser Herz gebildet; weder
unsre Hand gemacht, noch unser Leben berechnet. Blühen nicht unsre
Seelenkräfte ab, wie sie aufblühten? ja wechseln nicht mit Jahren und
Zuständen sie selbst unter einander und lösen im freundschaftlichen Zwist
oder vielmehr in einem kreisenden Reigentanz einander ab? Und wer
hätte es nicht erfahren, daß eine grenzenlose Ausbreitung seiner Empfindungen diese nur schwäche und vernichte? . . . Deine einzige Kunst, o
Mensch, hienieden ist also Maß: das Himmelskind, Freude, nach dem du
verlangst, ist um dich, ist in dir, eine Tochter der Nüchternheit und des
stillen Genusses, eine Schwester der Genügsamkeit und der Zufriedenheit
mit deinem Dasein im Leben und Tode.'[1]

[1] XIII. 339–40; 'Neither our hearts nor our heads are formed for an endlessly expanding fullness of thought and feeling. No more are our hands so made, nor our lives so intended. Will not
our spiritual faculties decline, just as they have flourished? Indeed, will they not all of them
change places with one another, with the different circumstances of the passing years, and
succeed one another, as it were in friendly rivalry or in the cyclical round of a dance? And
who cannot have learnt that an unlimited expression of his feelings weakens and destroys them?
. . . On this earth, O Man, your only art is measure: joy, the daughter of heaven, whom you
desire, is around you and within you, a daughter of sober activity and quiet pleasure, a sister
of sufficiency and contentment with your existence in life and death.'

Herder reverts to this thought again and again as the work progresses. It links him with the teachings of *Tasso*, of *Wilhelm Meister* and the completed *Faust*, as well as with the idealism of the Classical plays of Schiller.

The whole world is thus a school in which each must learn and cultivate that *Humanität* which is inherent, in embryo, within him. The all-wise headmaster is God Himself. The vehicle of education is tradition—the accumulated and transmitted experience of the race— which is brought into contact with the innate powers of the learner. Imperfection exists in the world in order that man, being conscious of it, may seek improvement; for Mephistopheles has his place in Herder's system in the same way as he has in Goethe's.

'Es gibt also eine Erziehung des Menschengeschlechts', Herder asserts in deliberate contradistinction to Lessing, 'eben weil jeder Mensch nur durch Erziehung ein Mensch wird und das ganze Geschlecht nicht anders als in dieser Kette von Individuen lebt. . . . Denn kein einzelner von uns ist durch sich selbst Mensch worden.'[1]

The channels by which this educative tradition is formed and com- municated are language, the state, and religion. In dealing with all these Herder was distinctly ill at ease. In the field of language he hankered after his naturalistic opinion of its origin, as set out in 1770, and it is as if only fear of Hamann prevented him from stating his real views. His treatment of religion is full of bitterness, for he saw its backslidings only too clearly.

Neither of these sections gave Herder so much trouble, however, as the chapter on the state, which, even after four revisions, ranges itself with Schiller's *Kabale und Liebe* in its violent condemnations. Assum- ing that all states are despotisms always, he found that they were the cause not of progress but of degradation and destruction. In an un- printed draft, he declared that man is born free and equal, needing no master, no government, unless he is weak and undeveloped. The modern state is totally unnatural, the only natural form of govern- ment being the national state, as the outcome of one national unit or group, and the complete expression of the national existence. Few of Herder's teachings have been more influential than this, the out- come of personal rancour and personal yearning. In his view, how- ever, even the national state must acknowledge its ultimate duty to be self-effacement, once it has assisted its citizens to govern themselves.

---

[1] XIII. 345-6; 'Thus, there is an education of mankind, precisely because each man only becomes a man through education and the whole race cannot live otherwise than as a chain of individuals. . . . For no one of us has become a man by his own efforts.'

With these sections, and an outline of the oldest Asiatic traditions concerning the beginnings of the earth, among which the Biblical account has the place of honour, the general introduction comes to an end. The real history now begins.

No reader of the *Ideen* can fail to admire the skilful and stimulating characterizations that fill the third and fourth parts. Never did Herder's powers of divination, penetration, and assimilation reveal themselves so brilliantly. Each nation is concisely and pregnantly delineated in turn. Herder's vision, like Goethe's, extends over all the infinite mutations of extant forms, so as to discover characteristics and set forth general principles. We see that each human phenomenon exists, not for the sake of some other phenomenon, but for its own sake, while all belong together within the grand unity of history. *Humanität*, in all its variety, as in all its oneness, is the balance in which every manifestation of the human spirit is weighed, and approved or rejected, while behind all things, guiding and sustaining, is seen the beneficient wisdom of God. On the factual side, Herder's ideal, no less than Goethe's, was:

> Daß du schauest, nicht schwärmst.[1]

'Die ganze Menschengeschichte', he wrote, 'ist eine reine Naturgeschichte menschlicher Kräfte, Handlungen und Triebe nach Ort und Zeit. . . . Das Schicksal offenbart seine Absichten durch das was geschieht und wie es geschieht; also entwickelt der Betrachter der Geschichte diese Absichten bloß aus dem, was da ist und sich in seinem ganzen Umfange zeigt.'[2]

It is ultimately on faith, however, that all Herder's history was founded. It was faith that gave it direction, force, conviction, urgency; faith, combined with the consuming longing to grasp, indeed merge with the manifestations of God and to seek comfort in them. The stimulus of science, as of so much in all German scientific investigation, lay not in reason but in feeling. Herder's religious belief had given birth to his philosophy of history; his philosophy of history now served to find evidence to strengthen this belief. More and more, as the years moved on, he lived a captive in the world of his faith, of his dreams, of his history. The Romantic basis of the *Ideen* bewitched their creator until there was no cranny of escape. His yearning fed upon its own visions.

The basis was Romantic, the result no less so. Elements that are

---

[1] Goethe, 'Metamorphose der Tiere'; 'That you shall see, not dream.'
[2] XIV. 145; 'The whole history of mankind is a pure natural history of the human faculties, actions, and impulses according to place and time. . . . Fate reveals its intentions by that which takes place and the manner in which it takes place. Thus the spectator of history finds out these intentions merely from that which exists and manifests itself in all its fullness.'

well known in Romanticism were comprised in it in abundance—
Hellenism, Orientalism, Medievalism, the theory of *race*, *moment*,
milieu, the ideas of continuity, of development, nationalism, and
many others. At the same time the picture was Classical too, as may
be seen in the conclusions Herder drew regarding human personality
and conduct. Indeed, while he foreshadowed doctrines of the
Romantic movement, there was nothing more in keeping with the
mature ideals of Goethe than the findings of the *Ideen*.

The contents of the historical sections arrange themselves easily.
As in his earlier philosophy, Herder explains each civilization according to its origin in native circumstances, in geographical and ethno-
logical conditions, and considers its manner of self-expression in
language, art, science, religion, and general culture. Everywhere he
strives to show and assess the value of what had of necessity to emerge,
and to point out the universal moral, for peoples as for individuals,
namely that each must fulfil nature's intentions, indeed co-operate
with her, by achieving what it is possible to achieve in given circumstances.

'Jeder strebe also auf seinem Platz, zu sein was er in der Folge der Dinge
sein kann; denn dies soll er auch sein und ein andres ist für ihn nicht
möglich.'[1]

It follows that the doctrine of nationalism appears again and again
as Herder proceeds. Drawing attention to inherited characteristics
which assist in determining national differences, he writes:

'Mit der veränderten Form eines menschlichen Kopfs und Gehirns, mit
Einer kleinen Veränderung im Bau der Organisation und der Nerven, die
das Klima, die Stammesart und die Gewohnheit bewirkt, ändert sich auch
das Schicksal der Welt, die ganze Summe dessen, was allenthalben auf
Erden die Menschheit tue und die Menschheit leide.'[2]

There can be no denying the historic significance of this renovation of
Pascal's allusion to Cleopatra's nose!

The Far Eastern countries, India, Persia, Judaea, Carthage, Egypt,
are characterized in turn, and the *Ideen* move towards their climax in
the analysis of Greek civilization, as the highest ever known. Herder's
task is to account for the origins of Greek achievement and to state the
lessons that moderns might learn from it. The requisite explanation

---

[1] XIV. 149; 'Thus, let each one strive in his own place to be what he can be in the whole
course of things. For this is what he must be; anything else is impossible for him.'

[2] XIV. 39; 'With the different form of a human head and brain, with one little difference
in the structure of man's physical and nervous system, effected by climate, heredity, and habit,
the destiny of the world is changed, the whole sum of that which mankind does and suffers
everywhere on earth.'

is found in the combination of hereditary and environmental circumstances. Out of these grew the glories of Greek mythology, poetry, music, art, ethics, politics. Herder then derives four major hypotheses from his study of Greece and they are the pillars upon which all his thought rests. These are:

1. 'Was im Reich der Menschheit nach dem Umfange gegebner National-, Zeit- und Ortsumstände geschehen kann, geschieht in ihm wirklich.'

2. 'Was von Einem Volk gilt, gilt auch von der Verbindung mehrerer Völker untereinander; sie stehen zusammen, wie Zeit und Ort sie band: sie wirken aufeinander, wie der Zusammenhang lebendiger Kräfte es bewirkte.'

3. 'Die Kultur eines Volks ist die Blüte seines Daseins, mit welcher es sich zwar angenehm, aber hinfällig offenbart.'

4. 'Die Gesundheit und Dauer eines Staats beruht nicht auf dem Punkt seiner höchsten Kultur sondern auf einem weisen oder glücklichen Gleichgewicht seiner lebendig-wirkenden Kräfte. Je tiefer bei diesem lebendigen Streben sein Schwerpunkt liegt, desto fester und dauernder ist er.'[1]

At the same time, the general conclusion is reached that those factors which are based upon *Humanität*—which is now synonymous with reason and equity, *Vernunft und Billigkeit*—alone have permanence and value, and the purpose of mankind is the manifestation and cultivation of this humane ideal.

It is an optimistic belief in the innate goodness of man and the wisdom inherent within the universe—a belief in what he termed *Licht, Liebe, Leben*—that underlies Herder's book. Historical evidence is made to prove that obedience to the laws of nature will secure the evolution of a system of human society in which the virtues of *Humanität* will prevail. *Humanität*—elusive term that it is—seems now to have become identical with happiness, as man's final goal.

It is easy to see that what Herder meant was that there are certain common principles of humanity and that they manifest themselves in different degrees according to individuality of time and place. The manner of his presentation, however, stresses the latter

---

[1] XIV. 144-9; 1. 'That which can come about in the realm of mankind within the compass of given national, temporal, and local conditions, really does come about.'
2. 'That which is true of one nation, is also true of the combination of several nations; they stand together just as time and place united them; they influence one another, just as the conjunction of vital forces has determined.'
3. 'The culture of a nation is the flower of its existence, in which it manifests itself as being pleasant but transitory.'
4. 'The health and longevity of a state are founded not upon its highest point of culture, but upon a wise or happy balance of its vitally operative faculties. The deeper its centre of gravity is within this living effort of its existence, the more stable and durable it is.'

aspect so much as to make it doubtful whether these common principles can function universally at all. He sets up his ideal, but in the same breath undermines its validity, or at least our faith in its validity, without really intending to do so. The crack in the structure gapes open before the structure is itself complete. Herder's followers widened it even more.

The implication existing in Herder's mind that his own country should reproduce the greatness that Greece achieved, though in a manner characteristic of itself, has, despite its inherent contradiction, launched German thought into ever more enticing paths. First one aspect and then another of this vague desire has been in the forefront, but never has the contradiction been discerned sufficiently clearly and enduringly as to lead to a re-orientation in favour of something more coherent. Instead, every effort has been consciously strained in the interest of this 'ideal', in total oblivion of Herder's own teaching that greatness is reached unconsciously. The basis of all this is a fatalistic belief, clearly implied by Herder, that once and once only does history grant the opportunity to a nation, so that every chance must be grasped lest the true one be let slip.

The lesson Herder teaches is the lesson of the *Fragmente*, only now it is accompanied by a note of mingled hope and despair.

'Laßt uns also, wenn wir selbst nicht Griechen sein können, uns wenigstens freuen, daß es einmal Griechen gegeben und daß ,wie jede Blüte der menschlichen Denkart, so auch diese ihren Ort und ihre Zeit zur schönsten Entwicklung fand. . . . Wir wollen sie schätzen lernen, ohne selbst Griechen zu werden.'[1]

Can Herder have had qualms about the outcome of his doctrine? Can he have been afraid of an attempt at their application by his own age and his own country?

It is a weakness that Herder based his conclusions upon ancient history alone. Modern history was for him a vast and formless unit without any clear divisions, and scarcely existed except as material with which to illustrate and corroborate the results he had already obtained; it did not, it seems, amend or invalidate them, whenever it failed to provide the necessary illustration! Thus, in contrast to Greek civilization, everything that came after, in Rome and the Middle Ages, appeared to Herder in the light of a setback to true progress. He saw darkness and decline and retrogression. Where

---

[1] XIV. 105; 'Therefore, if we cannot be Greeks ourselves, let us at least rejoice that there once were Greeks and that this flower of human thought, like every other, came at the time and place of its finest growth. . . . Let us learn to value it, without ourselves becoming Greeks.'

Gibbon was merely cynical, Herder struck a tragic note. The Roman
state, he declared, was foredoomed to destruction, for the seeds of
corruption were already present in its warlike spirit and its disunity.
Rome served him as a striking example of the law that evil can have
no other end than self-destruction. 'Das Gesetz der Wiedervergel-
tung ist eine ewige Naturordnung',[1] was Herder's oft-repeated
assertion. 'Alle Schuld rächt sich auf Erden',[2] wrote Goethe more
concisely. The thought is basically an application of Herder's idea
of Nemesis.

It is a major fault that Herder's conclusions were set forth long
before his history was finished. He followed his old method of
demonstrating and passing judgement, all in the same breath, in the
case of every historical phenomenon he discussed. That is how it came
about that there are almost imperceptible shiftings of emphasis and
variations of significance, until the reader finds that he has been moved
on to lines quite different to those on which he started. The process
is hard to analyse, until after the event, so convincing at the time is
the achievement.

The question arises as to whether, having reached his conclusions,
Herder needed to say more. He must have felt that the survey of
modern history was superfluous, or, if not superfluous, that it might
be broken off with impunity and concluded in a later work or works.
For that is what in fact happened. Herder's philosophy of history
strove to be at one and the same time a philosophy and a history.
It was finished as a philosophy before it was finished as a history, and
to write further history without adding essentially to the philosophy
seemed pointless. The substance, therefore, that did not get into the
Ideen, particularly into the projected fifth part, passed over into the
Zerstreute Blätter and *Humanitätsbriefe*, to be treated there from somewhat different angles.

The *Ideen* broke off in the middle of the medieval period, but not
until some fruitful characterizations had been presented. The chapter
on the Slavs, for instance, was one of the most influential in the whole
work, for Herder indicated a great future for this race.

Upon the value of Christianity for human development Herder
produced an account that is truly remarkable from the pen of a
minister of religion. Nothing more negatively rationalistic could be
imagined. It is a continuation of the double-edged verdict upon
religion in the second volume, where Herder had bewailed the

---

[1] XIV. 177; 'The law of requital is an eternal ordinance of nature.'
[2] Goethe, 'Wer nie sein Brot mit Tränen aß'; 'All guilt is punished on this earth.'

results of loss of faith. Like another Voltaire or Gibbon (the latter of whom he indeed defends!), he reveals the dark side of Christianity, its fanaticism, worldliness, obscurantism, tyranny, and destructive effect upon native originality. The restless movement of the early Middle Ages is admirably brought out, and though the picture is not now drawn with the glowing sympathy of *Auch Eine Philosophie*, the same factors—Chivalry, Love, Religion—that had so romantically enriched the earlier sketch dominate the scene once again. The value of this for the coming generation was prodigious. All the time, however, we feel that the vision is darkened by the sense of tragic decline that possessed Herder in face of his own age. Everything, we are made to feel, leads inevitably up to the contemporary troubles of the eighteenth century, and the Middle Ages suffered, therefore, as the progenitors of the corrupt present. At least Herder's logic and his bitterness coincided here, when he saw that a defective present could not have emerged from a faultless past. Herder's mockery reached its culminating point when he declared that the Arabs gave to Europe what the Church did not—science, poetry, legend, *Märchen*, romance —and filled the continent with new life. In words that were a revelation to his time, he asserted in a sweeping generalization that all modern literature goes back to Provençal origins, themselves the product of the transforming influence of Arab culture, with all its finer delicacies. Thence came the *gaya ciencia* of the Middle Ages. Thence, too, was derived the French domination of European civilization which lasted until Herder's own time. With the awakening of Europe that started in the unrest of the Crusades, occurred the first movements towards the liberation from the authority of Rome, Manicheism, Scholasticism, and Mysticism, until the revival of learning finally set all European civilization upon the basis of scientific effort.

In this work, as elsewhere, Herder was indebted to many forerunners; besides Spinoza, Leibniz, and Shaftesbury, to Montesquieu, Hume, and others. But no man had penetrated so deeply into the springs of human affairs, nor been so catholic in vision as he. There is scarcely anything in the world's history of which Herder does not take account, scarcely a possibility that he overlooks for the future. On this score alone, the book is still surprisingly refreshing and modern. For all its faults, and there are serious ones, it paved the way for later philosophies of history. To its extraordinary suggestiveness many branches of knowledge owe much of their present-day meaning and vitality, from astronomy, physics, and zoology to

geography, ethnology, and psychology. Herder laid particular stress
on the history of language and literature, and may justly be regarded
as the *fons et origo* of these studies in their modern sense.

The *Ideen* aroused almost universal admiration among contemporaries, for the book said what so many were thinking. *Humanität*
was the doctrine of the whole Classical movement and Herder was its
High Priest. The effect of his teaching was independent of its un-
sound logic. As Kant was quick to see, correctness of inference
yielded to divinations and unsupported fancies. It never even seems
to have occurred to Herder that an exact definition of *Humanität* was
needed. Its seductive vagueness appears to have deceived its chosen
exponent. It is, at once, both what man *has* achieved and the ideal of
what he *should* achieve. The most far-reaching contradiction of all is
that man is free, with his own individual purpose to fulfil, while being
at the same time a unit in the progress of the race, valued, not for
his own sake, but for what he adds to the course of civilization. The
idea of service and submission, in the last resort implying the negation
of individualism, follows logically from this latter point. In a wider
sense, the dualism of the idea of development and the idea of the
individual value of each phenomenon could not be harmonized, until
Hegel achieved the solution at the expense of history. Again, the
individual is declared to be a product of the interaction of his own
effort and of outside influence. Herder takes free will for granted but
hardly convinces us of its ability to function amid all the external and
inherited factors to which he proceeds to ascribe a decisive formative
effect. He has, thus, been repeatedly reproached for making man, as
Cousin put it, the 'child and passive scholar of nature'.

The trouble arose from Herder's strong pedagogic sense, from the
desire to criticize and to improve his own age, and ultimately,
therefore, from his own personal dissatisfaction. This clearly conflicted with the historical outlook, as it had done before. Herder was
always seeing deficiencies and striving to eliminate them, always seeking and never finding harmony between himself and the world. The
yearning for oneness with God-Nature was in his soul now as much
as ever before. The gulf between himself and his immediate surroundings strengthened his yearning and rendered objectivity quite
out of the question. As the work progressed, Herder's antipathy
became more and more acute, his resentment against his social and
political environment more and more deeply ingrained, and so the
sublime effort to view the whole of human history within the grand
scheme of the cosmos was vitiated by the polemical impulse, even

more, indeed, than the 1774 attempt had been. At the same time, the religious exaltation that had afforded at least some comfort in the earlier period had markedly receded, indeed partially given way to something akin to rationalist criticism. *Humanität* was now Herder's consolation in face of contemporary shortcomings; he clung to it with great—but not unshaken—optimism, and into it he projected the qualities he missed so much around him—peace, religion, sympathy, equity, reason, truth. He proclaimed his doctrine, which rested on personal longing, as if it were the law of nature.

Here is the reason for the appeal of the *Ideen*, as well as for their weakness—the ever-present personal note, the general romanticizing spirit that pervades the book. Herder approached his subject full of love and faith, overflowing with sympathetic understanding and ardent faith and idealism, ready to assimilate and praise everything that gave him spiritual nourishment and to extend it to his readers. Science and religious speculation are inextricably entangled, so that we are presented, not with a work of methodical exactitude, but with a vast poetic eulogium, highly fascinating and eminently influential. We are gripped by the aching desire to transform dreams into life. The enthusiasm that filled the author communicates itself to us. There is indeed a unity in the *Ideen* despite the disunity of details. It is a unity of mood. And it is founded ultimately upon an all-embracing faith in the omniscient wisdom of God-Nature.

This unity forms the real subject of the religious companion to the *Ideen*, the conversations on Spinoza, entitled *Gott* (1787). This is Herder's contribution to the famous Spinoza dispute which Jacobi had initiated, when he declared that Lessing had proclaimed himself to be a Spinozist. Herder, who had been acquainted with Spinoza at least since 1774, if not earlier, set out in these conversations to try to establish what Spinoza really meant—which is not the same thing as agreeing with him at every point—and to secure justice for him against the charge of atheism to which he was subjected. In 1786, in a letter to Gleim, he had announced himself as a 'Spinozist', but in this work he says just the reverse. He presumably meant that he was sympathetic to Spinoza without identifying himself with him. Herder's apology quickly becomes a presentation of his own philosophical beliefs, and it is hard to tell where the dividing-line comes. *Gott* resembles all Herder's works in this respect; they all set out to be interpretations, and imperceptibly they become expressions of his own views, as the pedagogic urge takes precedence over all else.

Turning upon the rationalist misinterpretation of Spinoza, Herder applies his usual genetical method; he explains the philosopher by means of his *milieu*, and finds that he was hampered by the Cartesian method and terminology. He proceeds, we feel, to draw Spinoza's conclusions for him, to free him from the limitations imposed by Cartesian dogma. He develops Spinoza's philosophy beyond the point at which Spinoza left it. He then uses him for the support and further elaboration of his own beliefs. He roundly declares the philosopher to be neither an atheist nor a pantheist. He asserts that pantheism is an error, and there is no word at all to suggest that Herder was himself a pantheist, as is sometimes assumed. As before, he adopts the methods of pantheism without accepting its doctrine. His God is transcendental, now as always. God is not the world and the world is not God. But the world *is* the expression of God, who is at once in and above all things. The philosophy is that of the study-scene and of the second garden-scene in *Faust*, and of Goethe's philo-sophical poems. The world is the 'living garment of God'—no more —a symbol of His greatness, always changing, growing, developing, never complete, and God, while not entirely the personal God of orthodox belief, is the God of order, the embodiment of the laws of the universe, through which He manifests Himself.

'Gott ist durch keinen Raum ausmeßbar, weil er mit keinem Dinge als Seines Gleichen coexistirt; er ist aber die ewige, unendliche Wurzel aller Dinge, so erhaben über unsere Einbildungskraft, daß in ihm aller Raum und alle Zeit verschwindet. Wir endliche Wesen, mit Raum und Zeit umfangen, die wir uns alles nur unter ihrem Maß denken, wir können von der höchsten Ursache nur sagen: sie ist, sie wirkt; aber mit diesem Worte sagen wir alles. Mit unendlicher Macht und Güte wirkt sie in jedem Punkt des Raums, in jedem Augenblick der forteilenden Zeit; Raum und Zeit aber sind nur uns ein dunkles oder helleres Bild vom Zusammenhange der Wesen nach jener festbestimmten ewigen Ordnung, welche die Eigen-schaft und Wirkung der unendlichen Wirklichkeit selbst ist, mithin auf nichts geringerm als dieser unteilbaren ewigen Unendlichkeit ruht.'[1]

---

[1] XVI. 488-9; 'God is not commensurable spatially, because He co-exists with nothing that is like Himself. But He is the eternal, infinite source of all things, and is so exalted beyond the power of our imagination, that in Him all space and time vanish. We finite beings, com-passed about by space and time, who conceive all things in these terms, can only say of the highest cause, "It is, it operates". But with these words we say everything. It operates with unending power and goodness in every point of space, in every moment of fleeting time. Space and time, however, are to us a more or less obscure image of the unity of all beings in accordance with that unshakably determined eternal order of things, which is the attribute and the outcome of that infinite reality itself, and thus is founded upon nothing less than this indivisible eternal infinity.'

Like Gretchen we say, and with her misgivings:

> Ungefähr sagt das der Pfarrer auch,
> Nur mit ein bischen andern Worten.[1]

It was easy for Jacobi and Kant to say that Herder misrepresented Spinoza, and combined pantheism with theism. The point is that Herder was presenting his own faith; Spinoza was merely his starting point. *Gott* is the complete gathering together of the religious doctrines on which his work—indeed the work of the whole Classical period—rests. The universe is regarded as a living system of forces, of cause and effect. God is present in every detail of life and growth. Creation is always going on. All is progress and development. Even evil exists to be in the service of good. A wise balance—Nemesis—presides over all the operations of the universe; and this is merely another aspect of divine omniscience and wisdom. Our faith is fostered by observing and reflecting upon the order of the things that God has made. We have no nobler duty. Science is the servant of religion.

Here, then, is the reason for Herder's study of history, the whole of history in all its aspects and manifestations. It is only the knowledge of God, of

> was die Welt
> Im Innersten zusammenhält,[2]

that enables us to master our fate and achieve our highest purpose. For we are both spectators and actors in the universe, and therein lies the complexity of our task. Like Lessing, Herder declares that it is more delightful to search for truth than to possess it, since ultimate truth is beyond us and we can only observe the externality of things.

'Die Erforschung der Wahrheit hat den größeren Reiz; das Haben derselben macht vielleicht satt und träge. Der Natur nachzugehen, ihre hohen Gesetze erst zu ahnen, dann zu bemerken, zu prüfen, sich darüber zu vergewissern, jetzt sie tausendfach bestätigt zu finden und neu anzuwenden; allenthalben endlich dieselbe weiseste Regel, dieselbe heilige Notwendigkeit wahrzunehmen, lieb zu gewinnen, sich selbst anzubilden; das eben macht den Wert eines Menschenlebens.'[3]

---

[1] *Faust*, 3460-1; 'Much the same way the preacher speaks,
        Only with slightly different phrases.'

[2] *Faust*, 382-3; 'The inmost force which binds the world.'

[3] XVI. 560; 'The search for truth has the greater charm; the possession of it may, perhaps, make us sated and indolent. To pursue nature, first to surmise her exalted laws, then to observe, test, and verify them, and now at this moment to find them confirmed a thousandfold, and then to apply them anew; finally, to perceive everywhere the same all-wise law, the same divine necessity, to come to love it, and to make it one's own, it is just this that gives human life its value.'

This Faustian philosophy is rounded off by the statement that it is in the full and practical use of all our life that we must know and enjoy God, and not in any more limited manner than that. Herder's intense desire for a life of action is elevated to the level of a burning religious belief.

There is here ample correction for any misconception that the Faustian faith was of secondary moment in the mid-Classical period. Nothing could speak more emphatically to the contrary than this remarkable book. It is known how enthusiastically it was received by Goethe—the Goethe who was in Italy and supposedly far removed from the outlook of his early years. Goethe resumed active work upon his *Faust* at this very time. He received *Gott* on his birthday, August 28, 1787, in Rome. He was following, as always, the progress of the *Ideen* with the keenest sympathy, having written from Naples on May 17, 1787, in anticipation of the third volume:

'Was mir auch von Dir begegnen wird und wo, soll mir willkommen sein; wir sind so nah in unsern Vorstellungsarten, als es möglich ist, ohne Eins zu sein, und in den Hauptpunkten am nächsten.'[1]

It was not by chance that the 'Wald und Höhle' scene came directly afterwards. The new plan of *Faust* emerged in February, 1788.

[1] 'Whatever may come to me from you, and wherever I may be, I shall welcome it. We are as near to one another in our views as is possible without being one person, and nearest of all in the major points.'

CHAPTER VIII

THE APPLICATION OF *HUMANITÄT*

HERDER'S eyes were turned in longing towards the past and towards the future. Greece was his ideal, supreme above all else. He was completely wrapped up in its greatness as a manifestation of *Humanität*. He could not speak of it sufficiently or praise its various achievements highly enough. He had already presented the essentials in the Greek chapter in the *Ideen*. He next proceeded to details, studying and translating lyrics and epigrams, and modernizing myths. He re-interpreted Greek doctrines to suit his own needs. All the time he looked forward to a modern revival that would be of comparable excellence. But nothing short of an unattainable reproduction of all the circumstances that brought about the one-time splendour of Greece would permit the desired revival. Herder's conception of the fatal causality inherent in history rendered impossible the very things he dreamed of most. History showed him wonderful vistas, only to reveal them as things that had been and could be no more. He was the victim of his own historical method. He yearned, he hoped, he dreamed. He spoke of a 'recurrence'—not altogether unlike Nietz-sche—only to reject it, as his doctrine of environment, growth, and heredity compelled him to do. He discussed the theory of reincarna-tion, only to cast it aside as implying the negation of all striving for betterment. He adapted his theory of palingenesis so as to supplement his dream of human regeneration, and at the same time entered into the problem of the after-life in order to set the seal upon his belief in the efficacy of striving in this world. Meanwhile, he never lost sight of the endless task of enlightening his country about itself and its native past, with a view to encouraging national self-consciousness and stimulating the revival he sought.

These subjects, along with his studies of the poetry, mythology, and antiquities of the East, of India and Persia, as well as translations of Persian lyrics, form the contents of the miscellaneous collection of *Zerstreute Blätter*, in which old and new material is included.

Political events, with the stagnation of Germany on the one hand and the apparent revival of France on the other, rendered Herder's task of regeneration all the more pressing. Even though at times he may seem to be divided against himself—and the dialogue form he uses so often is very symbolical of this—the constant theme, repeated again and again, is that there is no limit to what can be achieved by unremitting striving to fulfil the requirements of *Humanität*. Herder's teaching is that the pursuit of *Humanität* will bring about a re-birth of human culture on earth and gain the crown of supreme existence in the hereafter. The group of essays concerned with immortality—'Gespräche über die Seelenwanderung', 'Über die menschliche Unsterblichkeit', 'Tithon und Aurora', 'Palingenesie', 'Vom Wissen und Nichtwissen der Zukunft', are particularly significant in this connexion. Taken alone they are very attractive, but taken with Herder's other writings they are merely repetitive. In words that foreshadow the Romantic theory of Fichte and others, Herder paints a picture of earthly immortality, teaching that we must so live our lives, in accordance with the ideal of *Humanität*, that our achievements will live on in posterity, in exactly the same way as the best that we ourselves possess is a heritage from the past. Life goes on in an endless, progressive chain; we receive and we pass on; that is the eternal course of things.

Herder goes further. In 'Tithon und Aurora' he foresees a definite rejuvenation. He believes, it seems, in a periodical evolution in nature, in rhythmical revivals in which slumbering powers will awaken. That is how he finds satisfaction in face of contemporary futility. He elevates his belief in a revival to the status of a natural law, although it is not easy for him to reconcile this with the teachings of his own history. He speaks of 'palingenesis' or 're-birth', developing an idea that had occupied him since his youth.

'Der alte Mensch in uns soll sterben, damit eine neue Jugend emporkeime. . . . Nicht Revolution, aber eine glückliche Evolution der in uns schlummernden, uns neu-verjüngenden Kräfte. Was wir Überleben unsrer selbst, also Tod nennen, ist bei bessern Seelen nur Schlummer zu neuem Erwachen, eine Abspannung des Bogens zu neuem Gebrauche. So ruht der Acker, damit er desto reicher trage: so erstirbt der Baum im Winter, damit er im Frühling neu sprosse und treibe. Den Guten verläßt das Schicksal nicht, so lange er sich nicht selbst verläßt, und unrühmlich an sich verzweifelt.'[1]

In this ever-continuing renewal mankind's inheritance is eternally

---

[1] XVI. 122; 'The old man in us shall die, so that a new youth shall arise. . . . Not revolution but a happy evolution of the rejuvenating forces that slumber within us. What we call survival or death ,is in nobler souls merely a sleep before a new awakening, an unbending of the bow before it is used afresh. Thus, the cornfield rests so that it may bear the more richly; the tree dies in winter so that it may sprout and grow fresh shoots in the spring. Fate does not desert a good man so long as he does not desert himself and ingloriously lose heart.'

bursting forth afresh. Our task is to assist Providence by contributing to this process.

'Auf uns hat die Vorsehung gerechnet. . . . In diesem Leben ist also den Menschen Palingenesie, Metempsychose unentbehrlich; oder sie ist überhaupt mißlich. Denn was förderte den Fortgang des Menschen im Menschengeschlecht? und was hielt ihn zurück? Einzelne große und gute Menschen förderten ihn, die eine neue Geburt der Gedanken und Bestrebungen ans Licht brachten. Sie erschienen wie Genien und zwangen andre weiter.—Was hemmte hierauf den Fortgang, und machte daß jede neue Bildung immer nur rückweise geschah? Die Trägheit andrer Menschen. . . . Es muß also eine große Palingenesie der Gesinnungen unsres Geschlechts vorgehen, daß unser Reich der Macht und Klugheit auch ein Reich der Vernunft, Billigkeit und Güte werde.'[1]

Like Faust, when he says:

> Nach drüben ist die Aussicht uns verrannt;
> Tor! wer dorthin die Augen blinzelnd richtet . . .
> Er stehe fest und sehe hier sich um,[2]

Herder asserts that speculation about the hereafter is immaterial; we cannot know, only believe. It is this life and what we make of it that matters here.

'Nicht die Wissenschaft des Zukünftigen und die Spekulation über dasselbe ist die Lektion meines Lebens, sondern der Gebrauch des Gegenwärtigen. Dazu habe ich Mittel und Kräfte.'[3]

Once we feel, as Herder never did, that we have contributed something that will live and aid our fellow-men, we can doubtless declare ourselves satisfied, as Faust did in the end.

Palingenesis means, then, a purification and regeneration of our whole life in this world as a means of winning a higher than earthly life. We yearn to get beyond mortal imperfections and such yearning is ordained by Providence itself. Only the body is confined to the earth, the soul moves on to new and more exalted spheres. There is a

---

[1] XVI. 352-6; 'Providence has counted upon us. . . . In this life, therefore, re-birth or metempsychosis is indispensable; else it is altogether something doubtful. For what has furthered the progress of man and what has held him back? Great and good individuals have furthered him, for they produced a re-birth of thought and endeavour. They came forth like geniuses and urged others forward. What hindered progress afterwards and made each new growth retrogressive? The indolence of other men. . . . Therefore there must take place a great re-birth in the sentiments of our race, so that our kingdom based on power and expediency may become a kingdom based on reason, equity, and goodness.'

[2] *Faust*, II. 11442-5; 'The view beyond is barred immutably;
A fool who there his blinking eyes directeth!
He here acquires what he can apprehend.'

[3] XVI. 370; 'It is not knowledge of the hereafter and speculation about it that is the lesson my life teaches, but the use of the present. It is for that I have the means and the powers.'

gradation of being in the universe, and each phase must be passed through in its turn.

'Sehen Sie die große Leiter, die alles hinaufklimmt, und den weiten Weg, den wir noch zu machen haben, ehe wir zum Mittelpunkt und Vaterlande dessen kommen, was wir nur in unserm Sternensystem Wahrheit, Licht, Liebe nennen.'[1]

At this point Herder adds to what he has already taught us about the outlook of *Faust* by remarks that elucidate the meaning of Eros in Goethe's poem. We cannot, he declares, fulfil our existence in ourselves alone, but only in striving for some object outside ourselves, whether it be God or some other being whom we love. The act of giving and receiving, of surrendering ourselves in order to find ourselves again, as Herder describes it, is clearly in its essence the same as the 'drawing-onward' (the *Hinanziehen*) of Faust by the power of love, on earth and in the after-life. The essay 'Über Liebe und Selbstheit', whose starting-point was Hemsterhuis' *Lettres sur les désirs* (which Herder translated), concludes with the significant words:

'So sind wir in diesem Weltall; und wie gehts auf unsrer ewigen Reise weiter hinauf? Schwerlich anders. Nur auf unserm eignen Dasein und Bewußtsein ruht die Existenz andrer, so fern sie durch Liebe und Sehnsucht mit uns verknüpft sind; verlören wir jene, so hätten wir auch von diesen keinen Genuß mehr. Notwendig wird unsre Existenz von Stufe zu Stufe immer freier und wirkender werden: unser Genuß wird weniger verderben und zerstören; wir werden immer mehr Freuden schmecken lernen, indem wir geben und tun, als indem wir nehmen und leiden. Indessen scheint das gegenseitige Verhältnis nie ganz aufhören zu können, das die Summe dieses ganzen Glücks macht. Um zu geben, müssen immer Gegenstände sein, die da nehmen; um zu tun, andre, für die man tue; Freundschaft und Liebe sind nie möglich, als zwischen gegenseitigen freien, konsonen, aber nicht unisonen, geschweige identifizirten Geschöpfen. Und was endlich den Genuß des höchsten Wesens anbetrifft; o da bleibts immer "Hyperbel mit ihrer Asymptote," wie unser Autor (Hemsterhuis) sagt, und muß es bleiben. Die Hyperbel nähert sich der Asymptote, aber sie erreicht sie nie: zu unsrer Seligkeit können wir nie den Begriff unsres Daseins verlieren, und den unendlichen Begriff, daß wir Gott sind, erlangen. . . . Wir nahen uns der Vollkommenheit, unendlich vollkommen aber werden wir nie.'[2]

---

[1] XV. 276; 'Look at the great ladder which all scale, and the long way we have still to go before we reach the centre and the fatherland of that which in our universe we can only call truth, light, love.'

[2] XV. 325-6; 'That is how our life is in this world; and how will it be on our eternal journey upwards? Hardly different. The existence of others rests only upon our life and our consciousness in so far as they are joined to us in love and longing. If we lost life and consciousness, we

The affinity between Herder's thought and that of *Faust*, which we have noted so often, reaches its peak at this time, the years of the closest friendship with Goethe, and it is permissible to see in Herder's theory of earthly and heavenly palingenesis a satisfactory commentary upon the riddle of the conclusion to Goethe's poem. Earthly immortality by means of what is achieved, then salvation through love, mortal and divine, the enduring retention of individuality, the never-ending striving, in the hereafter as well as now—that is the final teaching of this important essay of Herder.

One may also discern in Helena and in her purifying influence the incarnation of the doctrine of measure, of Nemesis, that Herder preached. Indeed, did he not find Nemesis to be identified by the Greeks with Leda or Helena? 'Es fürchte die Götter das Menschengeschlecht'[1] was his belief as well as Iphigenie's. It was a belief that not only was significantly applied in the sphere of history, but was also responsible for a crisis on the personal side. The key to Herder's own tragedy, no less than Faust's, lies in the inability fully to reconcile divinely ordained striving with a just measure. The problem of self-culture involved a degree of self-consciousness that in the last resort verged closely upon egoism. The balance was very difficult to hold. The lines—

> Vergiß dein Ich; Dich selbst verliere nie.
> Nichts Größres konnt' aus ihrem Herzen dir
> Die reiche Gottheit geben, als Dich selbst[2]—

pose the dilemma, and indicate its solution. It was Werther's and Tasso's dilemma as well as Herder's. It was the problem that the whole of the Classical movement strove to solve.

Herder ransacked the past and its literature for illustrations of his ideal. Greece, Persia, India, the Middle Ages—he knew them all.

---

should derive no more pleasure from others. Our existence will become necessarily more and more free and efficacious from stage to stage, our pleasure will be less perishable and less destructive; we shall learn more and more to savour the joy of giving and doing rather than of taking and being passive. Meantime, the mutual relationship which makes the sum of all our happiness, seems never to be susceptible of ceasing altogether. In order to give, there must always be objects that receive; in order to do, there must always be others for whom one does things; friendship and love are never possible except between mutually free creatures, living in harmony, but not in unison, much less identity. And concerning the enjoyment of the Highest Being, it is, and must be, a case of a "hyperbola with its asymptote," as our author (Hemsterhuis) puts it. The hyperbola approaches the asymptote, but never touches it. For our happiness, we can never lose the notion of our existence, and never attain to the infinite notion that we are God. . . . We approach perfection, but we never become infinitely perfect.'

[1] 'Let mankind fear the gods.'
[2] XXIX. 139; 'Forget yourself but never lose yourself.
No greater gift could e'er be made to you
From God's abundant heart than of yourself.'

His vision was limitless. He wrote on Persepolis, on *Sakontala*, on Greek myth and lyric, but, as he worked, it was not long before his old love, the German past, filled his heart again. He provided a stimulating sketch of the history of German literature, regretting his country's ignorance about its own past, demanding *inter alia* the publication of the Jena codex of Middle High German lyrical poetry, with which he himself was well acquainted. He discussed, with enthusiasm, *Reineke Fuchs*, having watched Goethe's renovation of this poem with interest; he praised Hans Sachs and discovered Andreä and Weckherlin. Like the Hutten he so much admired, Herder was to the end a great patriot and fighter for the enlightenment of his fellow-countrymen about themselves, their past, their hidden possibilities. His patriotism was an integral part of his all-embracing doctrine of *Humanität*. It rested on the same foundations. Self-culture meant for him the self-culture of nations as well as of individuals. He saw the same laws of nature in operation in each case, and the same dilemma was present. Striving, yearning, moderation, immortality applied equally to both.

In the midst of these writings there occurred the French Revolution, with the apparent possibility it brought in its train of transforming the sovereignty of reason and equity into reality. It seemed that an unheard of cultural re-birth might indeed be at hand, and it is not surprising that Herder's sympathy should have been at once aroused. Immediately before the outbreak of the Revolution he had been drafting, at the request of the Margrave of Baden, the programme for an 'Institute of National Enlightenment'. This was a congenial task, since Herder's patriotism invariably took a cultural form. He had found little real vitality in the miniature despotisms he had encountered since the Riga days, and still looked back with longing at the public spirit that had formerly impressed him in that city. He entertained hopes that the *Fürstenbund* might foster the national consolidation he had in mind, though, fundamentally, he was antagonistic to monarchical institutions, even to the state altogether. Democracy lay nearest to his heart. It is not surprising that scandal soon accused him of republicanism.

The first draft of the *Briefe zu Beförderung der Humanität* contained ample foundation for this charge. Herder looked upon the Revolution as completing the Reformation, inasmuch as it added to the demolition of clerical supremacy that of feudal privilege. He considered the people as a whole, not any particular class or party or sect, as the true basis of the state. The Revolution seemed to him to mark a new

epoch, therefore, and the golden era of political freedom that was
dawning ought, if he were to go by the analogy of Greece, to usher
in a new age of intellectual achievement that might even rival that
of Athens. Never before had the auspices been so favourable. The
only doubt was whether foreign intervention might not destroy the
glowing prospects of the Republic.

Herder was accordingly more than ever concerned that true
national idealism should grow up in Germany, and that she should
not be left behind in this imminent revival. He felt his position as a
teacher more and more acutely, and his duty was daily ever more
compelling. Just as, twenty years earlier, it had been his task to point
out the sources of the national revival in literature, so now he had the
wider obligation of inculcating the spirit of *Humanität* which was
to be the real foundation for the future.

This he attempts in the final (the published) form of the letters, the
disappointing developments in France having by this time made his
work even more urgent than before. Indeed, these developments
led him now to pin his faith almost exclusively on cultural rather
than political matters. Never can a man have striven to declare his
teaching in more distressing circumstances. He was ailing, had no
leisure for reflection, and was now horrified by the violence of the
Revolution he had welcomed so enthusiastically. So long as it did
away with old prejudices he favoured it, and indeed even regarded
the French resistance to the invading powers as the first example in
history of a holy and just war. But his dearest hopes had been
quickly shattered. He saw the world in the grip of irrational, demonic
forces—forces that he had once proclaimed as the origins of all true
creation but now condemned as they transgressed more and more the
law of measure that was his one refuge. He still dreamed, to be sure,
that something good might emerge from the ruins.

'Kein Übel, das der Menschheit begegnet, kann und soll ihr anders als
ersprießlich werden. Es läge ja selbst an ihr, wenn es ihr anders als ersprießlich würde: denn auch Laster, Fehler und Schwachheiten der Menschen
stehen als Naturbegebenheiten unter Regeln, und sind oder sie können
berechnet werden.'[1]

He still possessed a little of the optimism he inherited from his age.
For a moment we hear the voice, it seems, of Epictetus-Montaigne,

---

[1] XVII. 122; 'No evil that befalls man, can and shall be any other than salutary to him. It
would be his fault indeed, if it were any other than salutary; for even vices, faults, and weaknesses of man are, as happenings of nature, subject to nature's ordinances and are or can be
calculable.'

saying 'que le goust des biens et des maux depend en bonne partie de l'opinion que nous en avons'. Only Herder found Stoicism more difficult than most men to apply in his own case!

Out of fear of the censorship, Herder had to restrain his public utterance. He speaks of history, philosophy, poetry, art, but only slyly hints at politics. He adopts the form of a fictitious correspondence to 'ventilate' rather than decide awkward questions. In his difficulties he flees into the past, into the Middle Ages, into Greece, into the atmosphere of the primitive (and, incidentally, condemns slavery). His fatalism breaks down at this point. Events cause him no longer to accept all things as the work of the incomprehensible hand of Providence. He is completely at loggerheads with what is around him. At times he is objective and sees clearly what can and what can not be; mostly, however, he clings to his longing for what reality shows to be impossible. He lives more and more with his dreams. He speaks vaguely and indirectly and in parables. His history, had he consistently adhered to the pessimistic determinism of 1774, should have taught him that no good could come of an age he condemned. But he was filled with a dreamy longing to the contrary, only to see it constantly disappointed. Actuality proved the truth of those very conclusions of his own which he did not dare to accept. Never was a tragedy so bitter. Faith and yearning had thrown aside the pessimism of *Auch Eine Philosophie* and erected the seductive philosophy of *Humanität*; and now this teaching failed its creator in the critical test. Faced with stern reality, even the One True Prophet of the new doctrine was utterly at a loss. Yet he clung wishfully to his faith to the end.

To make up for the shortcomings of the present, Herder turns once again to the past. History is his solace as well as his teacher. He speaks of a visionary 'League of Humanity', a *Humanitätsbund*, which includes not only existing peoples of the world but all ages of history, all indeed who contribute or have contributed to human civilization. Poets and artists, as the greatest humanizing agents, the spokesmen and educators of mankind, have a prominent place in this. He proceeds to allow members of his grandiose confederation to declare their beliefs; Franklin, Frederick the Great (oddly enough), Luther, Comenius, Leibniz, Lessing are accordingly quoted at length. Herder returns in the course of all this to his starting-point in authorship and re-applies many of his early ideas in a fresh sense. Poetry, he declares, is the universal language in which all can speak to one another; its kingdom knows no limits of time or place, and past and present are united in its fellowship. It competes with Christianity as a civilizing agent.

'Wenn Poesie die Blüte des menschlichen Geistes, der menschlichen Sitten, ja ich möchte sagen das Ideal unsrer Vorstellungsart, die Sprache des Gesamtwunsches und Sehnens der Menschheit ist: so, dünkt mich, ist der glücklich, dem diese Blüte vom Gipfel des Stammes der aufgeklärtesten Nationen zu brechen vergönnt ist. . . . In dieser Rücksicht nun kann man freilich die Geschichte der Dichtkunst d.i. die Geschichte menschlicher Einbildungen und Wünsche, und wenn ich so sagen darf, des süßen Wahns der Menschheit, der aufs feurigste ausgedrückten Leidenschaften und Empfindungen unsres Geschlechts nicht allgemein und im Großen gnug nehmen. . . . Sie in diesem angenehmen Irrgarten zu belauschen, den Proteus zu fesseln und redend zu machen, den man gewöhnlich National-charakter nennt und der sich gewiß nicht weniger in Schriften als in Gebräuchen und Handlungen der Nation äußert; dies ist eine hohe und feine Philosophie. In den Werken der Dichtkunst d.i. der Einbildungskraft und der Empfindungen wird sie am sichersten geübt, weil in diesen die ganze Seele der Nation sich am freisten zeigt.'[1]

No wonder Mephistopheles cries out

Assoziiert euch mit einem Poeten[2]

when Faust demands to know the whole realm of human experience! The age must, therefore, not neglect its rich heritage, but treasure it for the fundamental truths of humanity which it embodies. Further-more, to study the cultures of other nations will serve the double purpose of pointing the way to national individuality and of promot-ing international solidarity. Indeed, Herder's conception of *Weltli-teratur*, which was more strongly developed in these years than ever, did not exclude, however universal in tendency it was, but emphatic-ally required, the cultivation of national self-expression in the fullest possible sense, so long as this represented—as it must, if it obeyed the law of nature—the essential qualities of humanity such as he had outlined, and which had been most perfectly exemplified in ancient Greece.

---

[1] XVIII. 57–8; 'If poetry is the flower of the human spirit and human culture, and indeed, as it were, the ideal of our imagination, the speech expressing all the desire and longing of mankind, so, I think, that man is happy who is permitted to pluck this bloom from the top of the stem of the most enlightened nations. . . . Now in this connexion one cannot take in too general and wide a sense the history of poetry, i.e. the history of human fancies and desires, and, if I may say so, of the silly-sooth notions of mankind, the most ardently expressed passions and feelings of our race. . . . To overhear these things in this pleasant labyrinth of a world, to chain and to interrogate the Proteus which is usually called national character and which manifests itself no less in writings than in usages and actions, this is a noble and fine philo-sophy. It is practised with greatest certainty in the works of poetry, i.e. of imagination and feeling, because in these the entire soul of a nation reveals itself most freely.'

[2] *Faust*, 1789; 'Go, league thyself with a poet!'

Herder's total ideal was a future federation made up of members all of whom had evolved in accordance with this natural law, all equal and perfectly self-developed nationalities, each with complete freedom to immortalize itself by making to the common cause its own individual contribution, its own particular realization of *Humanität*. Each must, therefore, strive in its own way towards the truth, and each will necessarily be drawn into harmonious co-operation with its fellows because of the basic qualities they all possess in common. In all things there is 'eine unendliche Verschiedenheit, zu einer Einheit strebend, die in allen liegt, die alle fördert'.[1] The local and the universal in humanity are fused together. The cracks in Herder's structure are covered up. The final function of nationalism is seen to be the main pillar in the temple of humanity.

Herder's presentation of examples of past achievement imperceptibly becomes once again an outline, though not indeed a history, of world culture, an outline, however, with a marked bias. He defines *Humanität* in more precise terms than formerly as

'der Charakter unsres Geschlechts; er ist uns aber nur in Anlagen angeboren, und muß uns eigentlich angebildet werden. Wir bringen ihn nicht fertig auf die Welt mit; auf der Welt aber soll er das Ziel unsres Bestrebens, die Summe unsrer Übungen, unser Wert sein: denn eine Angelität im Menschen kennen wir nicht, und wenn der Dämon, der uns regiert, kein humaner Dämon ist, werden wir Plagegeister der Menschen. Das Göttliche in unserm Geschlecht ist also Bildung zur Humanität; alle großen und guten Menschen, Gesetzgeber, Erfinder, Philosophen, Dichter, Künstler, jeder edle Mensch in seinem Stande, bei der Erziehung seiner Kinder, bei der Beobachtung seiner Pflichten, durch Beispiel, Werk, Institut und Lehre hat dazu mitgeholfen. Humanität ist der Schatz und die Ausbeute aller menschlichen Bemühungen, gleichsam die Kunst unsres Geschlechts. Die Bildung zu ihr ist ein Werk, das unablässig fortgesetzt werden muß; oder wir sinken, höhere und niedere Stände, zur rohen Tierheit, zur Brutalität zurück.'[2]

[1] XVIII. 300; 'An endless variety, striving for a unity that lies in all things and which urges all things forward.'
[2] XVII. 138; '. . . the character of our race; it is, however, inherited only as a natural predisposition; it must actually be inculcated. We do not bring it with us ready-made; but it must be the goal of our endeavour in the world, the sum of all our efforts, our whole value. For we do not know of men possessing the character of the angels; and if the daimon that rules us is not a human daimon, we become tormentors of mankind. That which is divine in our race is, thus, education for *Humanität*; all great and good men, lawgivers, inventors, philosophers, poets, artists, every noble-minded man, in his own station, in the education of his children, in the observance of his duties, by his example, his work, his tuition, and his teaching, has collaborated towards that end. *Humanität* is the treasure and the product of all human endeavours, as it were the whole art of the life of our race. Education for it is a work that must be continued without ceasing; or we shall sink back, higher and lower classes alike, to uncultured bestiality and brutality.'

As before, Herder is painfully aware of the discrepancy between his own age and that of Greece and moves at this time near to Schiller (who greatly admired Herder's observations on this point) and to Hölderlin, for both *Über naive und sentimentalische Dichtung* and *Hyperion* were concerned with this same theme. He takes his standards from Greece; they affect his judgement all along the line. To be sure, he also lays bare, once again, the driving forces of medieval literature, the *Liebe, Andacht,* and *Tapferkeit*[1] that delighted the Romanticists so much; and, like Novalis, he regards the Middle Ages as a great European confederacy, only he now censures their lack of measure, form, and dignity, qualities which were not supplied until the revival of Classical learning during the Renaissance.

Herder's literary analyses are novel and stimulating. He finds that while Catholic countries adhered to old literary ways, Protestant countries struck out in fresh directions and provided the world with poets who were not only minstrels but also philosophers. Shakespeare stood on the threshold of the new movement, combining both types in himself. The old judgements of the Shakespeare-essay of 1773 now emerge substantially as before, but in a striking context.

'Er steht zwischen der alten und neuen Dichtkunst, als ein Inbegriff beider da. Die Ritter- und Feenwelt, die ganze englische Geschichte, und so manch anderes interessantes Märchen lag vor ihm aufgeschlagen; er braucht, erzählt, handelt sie ab, stellt sie dar mit aller Lieblichkeit eines alten Novellen- und Fabeldichters. Seine Ritter und Helden, seine Könige und Stände treten in der ganzen Pracht ihrer und seiner Zeit vor, die in so manchen Gesinnungen, und dem ganzen Verhältnis der Stände gegen einander uns jetzt wie eine aus den Gräbern erstehende Welt vorkommt. . . . In dem allen ist er ein darstellender Minstrel, der Personen, Auftritte, Zeiten gibt, wie sie sich ihm gaben, und zu seinem Zweck dienten. Nun aber wenn er in diesen Szenen der alten Welt uns die Tiefen des menschlichen Herzens eröffnet, und im wunderbarsten, jedoch durchaus charakteristischen Ausdruck eine Philosophie vorträgt, die alle Stände und Verhältnisse, alle Charaktere und Situationen der Menschheit beleuchtet, so milde beleuchtet, daß allenthalben das Licht aus ihnen selbst zurückzustrahlen scheint: da ist er nicht nur ein Dichter der neueren Zeit, sondern ein Spiegel für theatralische Dichter aller Zeiten.'[2]

[1] 'Love, religion, bravery.'
[2] XVIII. 101-2; 'He stands halfway between ancient and modern poetry as an epitome of both. The world of chivalry and of fairyland, the whole of English history, and so many interesting romances lay open before him; he uses these, narrates and discusses them, presents them with all the pleasantness of an old poet who writes stories and myths. His knights and heroes, his kings and social classes, emerge in all the splendour of their age and his, which appears to us now, in so many of its sentiments and in the relationship of the classes to one another, like a world resurrected from the dead. . . . In all that, he is a minstrel who depicts,

For Herder, Shakespeare began the movement that led up to the novel, and what Herder says on the vast, all-embracing nature of this genre, its parallel with the epic of ancient times, and its endless scope and possibilities, foreshadows closely what Friedrich Schlegel (who reviewed the *Humanitätsbriefe*) wrote two years later on the novel as the expression of *Romantische Universalpoesie*. In the same way, Herder's survey of Greek literature anticipated that same writer's essays on the Greeks, and his history of European literature prepared the way for the comprehensive accounts to be given by both the Schlegel brothers. Indeed, there are times when the *Humanitätsbriefe* read surprisingly like a manifesto of Romanticism, if without its acute formulations. There is the same antithesis of North and South, of Ancient and Modern, of Greek and German, that had originated in the *Fragmente*. It only needs sharper definition and more expressive terminology for this to be turned into the Classic-Romantic antithesis. There is the same fusion of cosmopolitanism with nationalism, the same stock-taking of all available literature up to date. Of Germany, Herder declares that its language is unrivalled for translation purposes, and its literature is not formless, nor characterless, nor lacking in criticism. It merely requires to learn to know its powers, to absorb from others only what is fruitful, and to give up the absurd 'gallicomania' that has dogged it since the age of Louis XIV.

The *Briefe* end with a condemnation of the sectarianism of Kant's followers (containing, as a counterblast, a generous eulogy of the philosopher) and an alinement of Christianity with *Humanität*. The *Christliche Schriften* develop this last point further, and complete the picture of Herder's final philosophy. They represent his next, and perhaps most significant, effort to illustrate his ideal. From beginning to end the foundation of all his thought was religious, and in these writings his tenets are set out in their clearest and least provocative form, without any of the mystical trappings of the Bückeburg years. He begins, characteristically, with philological and historical essays in Biblical interpretation, attempting to find out what the Bible really means by reference to contemporary circumstances and beliefs. He goes on to supply detailed studies of the genesis and purposes of the Gospels and their arrangement in probable order of composition. However, as the work progresses, Herder's general beliefs and desires

who presents characters, scenes, and epochs, as they presented themselves to him and served his purpose. Now if, however, in these scenes of the past he plumbs the depths of the human heart for us, and in the most wonderful yet quite characteristic speech presents a philosophy which sheds light upon all classes and conditions, all characters and situations of mankind, so generously that everywhere the light seems to be radiated back again, then he is not only a poet of modern times, but a mirror for dramatic poets of all times.'

quickly emerge and get the upper hand of philology. It is always so. An objective beginning leads, as the writer falls more and more under the spell of what he says, to a personal declaration of faith.

Herder's interpretation of St. John's Gospel (1797) is worthy of attention because of its relation to corresponding material in Goethe's *Faust*, on which work was resumed in this same year. It is instructive, despite the alienation between Goethe and Herder, to turn to the latter for some elucidation, for there is nothing to show that Goethe returned the boycott to which Herder subjected *his* ideas. Herder pointed out the meaning of 'logos' to be 'wisdom', 'will', 'understanding', as well as 'word', declaring:

'Denn Geist und Wort sind bei den Ebräern eins; der Hauch vom Munde Gottes ist Wort, das Wort vom Munde Gottes ist Geist.'[1]

Nature is, thus, 'eine lebendige Ausrichterin seines Worts'.[2] As Faust says:

Im Anfang war der Sinn.[3]

When Herder describes *Vernunft*, God's gift to man, as 'ein Strahl des ewigen Lichts, ein inneres Leben aus der höchsten Quelle des Lebens',[4] the verbal parallel is again significant. There is more to come, largely, it must be said, anticipated in earlier writings, but now precisely stated, and with theological authority. God, we hear, regards the enlightenment of mankind as His own affair, just as He does in the 'Prologue in Heaven'. He stakes all upon His gift, *Vernunft*, for this alone will lead man to the truth, and the truth alone will make man free.

'Gewohnheit, Parteilichkeit, Eigennutz, Eigensucht, eitle Ehre, Wollust und Trägheit machen uns zu Sklaven jedes Unrechts, das wir zuletzt wissentlich tun müssen. Nur Wahrheit ist die Befreierin der Menschen; sie müssen wir als eine Stimme Gottes ganz erkennen wollen, oder die Frechheit selbst führt ihre Strafe mit sich,'[5]

writes Herder, in terms reminding us of Faust's

Wie ich beharre, bin ich Knecht.[6]

---

[1] XX. 74; 'For spirit and word are one and the same thing for the Hebrews; the breath from God's lips is the Word, the Word from God's lips is spirit.'

[2] XX. 120; 'A living executrix of His Word.'

[3] *Faust*, 1229; 'In the Beginning was the Thought.'

[4] XIX. 297; 'A ray of the eternal light, an inward life that comes from the highest source of all life.'

[5] XIX. 324; 'Habit, prejudice, selfishness, self-interest, empty honour, sensual pleasure, and indolence make us slaves to every form of wrong, which in the end we knowingly commit. Only truth can set man free, we must desire to acknowledge her entirely as the voice of God, or else presumption will come along bringing her own punishment with her.'

[6] *Faust*, 1710; 'A slave am I whate'er I do' (i.e. if I adhere to a mode of life such as the present one, which is stagnant).

Man's duty is to strive, not in selfish seclusion or for selfish ends, but in a spirit of untiring service and self-sacrificial love. Nature in all her ways can teach us that this is God's intention, if only we have eyes to see and reason with which to understand. Enlightenment and the leading of man to the full knowledge and application of his powers and destiny, to the recognition of his place and function, and his willing self-subjection to the law of the universe—this is Herder's programme. If mankind is unhappy, it is because it has failed to grasp or carry out God's will. For man is inherently good, and all the means of happiness have been granted to him.

Here is the background of *Faust*. It is a positive doctrine, the Kingdom of God upon earth, to be achieved by mankind through incessant, selfless striving in love and faith. It is Herder's answer to the political, social, and ethical troubles of the times, the theologian's retort to the new morality of the Kantian philosophy. Like Schleiermacher, he was concerned with the essential bases of religion, not with dogma. The scientific value of these writings may be small, but their importance for Herder himself, whose philosophy they rounded off, was great. Nothing in his whole work brings out so clearly the serene Herder of Graff's famous portrait, serene in the beauty of his longing.

There was little serenity in his immediate sphere. He found none of the peace and harmony around him that he sought so much. He was at war with Kant, Goethe, and Schiller, and the few years left to him were full of the intensest bitterness. Having arrived at his final philosophy, amply verified by history and religion, he was not disposed to tolerate any creed that conflicted with it. He who had found the truth regarded himself as a sort of censor. He was intolerant, pugnacious, indefatigable to the very end. His main work was finished. His age had left him behind. Reiteration of his beliefs to hostile ears brought only desolation and despair.

In particular, the herculean effort to refute the philosophy of Kant now occupied him almost to the exclusion of all else. It failed, as it was bound to do. He vainly hoped that he would complete a major reform in his age by ridding it of the new philosophy. The *Humanitätsbriefe* had already attacked sectarian dogmatism and the *Christliche Schriften* had, like the Lord in *Faust*, condemned the Kantian view that man was 'radically evil'.

The *Metakritik zur Kritik der reinen Vernunft* showed Herder to be utterly incapable of understanding his opponent. His whole approach was different. He could not see that the philosopher was seeking an

objective basis for knowledge. Kant's analyses all seemed so unneces-
sary to him; he was so secure in his own faith. We need only see,
grasp, believe. That had been his constant teaching. He would hear
of nothing that did not belong to experience. The antithesis of
thought and nature, of freedom and causality was something that
had no place in his monistic system. Thought was simply part of
nature, and its highest development the perception and understanding of nature, and therefore of God. The *Ding an sich* was, thus, not
unknowable; it could be known, though not perfectly, except by
God. In the sphere of ethics Herder would accept no other mode
of behaviour than obedience to the laws of nature, i.e. of God; Kant's
rejection of this in favour of the 'moral law' amounted in his eyes to
nothing less than blasphemy. He blamed the scepticism of Hume
for this Kantian error.

Despite their hostile reception—and the *Metakritik* had the widest
circulation of any of Herder's works—these views were soon to be
developed further and more productively by the nature-philosophy
of Schelling and the idealism of Hegel. Herder himself ignored the
attacks made upon him and went on to write his *Kalligone*, the
answer to the *Kritik der Urteilskraft*. He believed that it was Kant's
aesthetic theory, through Schiller (who in turn had infected Goethe),
that was leading German literature astray into paths of doubtful
artistic and moral value. However, his own approach is ultimately
not a refutation of, but a useful supplement to, Kant's position. Here
again he cannot believe that any abstract definition is needed of what
is self-evident to him. In the *Humanitätsbriefe* he had declared beauty
to be the external manifestation of goodness, placing the main emphasis on the ethical rather than on the aesthetic aspect of things. His
standpoint is naturalistic, founded upon sense-perception and upon
the pleasure—not a 'disinterested' pleasure, as Kant held—that the
senses feel in apprehending what is in itself harmonious and complete.
Beauty has a dual nature; it reposes in the object itself and in the
spectator, who projects his feelings into the object he observes. The
universe is beautiful, and all perfectly developed beings feel pleasure
in its appearance. We cannot assume an 'indifferent' or 'disinterested'
attitude towards beauty.

Herder made his final effort to illustrate his ideal in his periodical,
Adrastea. It was intended to make known the teachings of history
by means of a series of examples, and, in so doing, to demonstrate,
as the title suggests, the operation of the law of measure and to judge
the achievement of the eighteenth century in the light of this law.

The whole field of human effort is surveyed, from philosophy to missionary work, from politics to music, from freemasonry to literary theory. The work has indeed been aptly called a collection of 'crumbs from earlier meals'. But it is often no more than a diffuse and tiresome Jeremiad, despite much that is of value. Like the disgruntled old Author in the 'Walpurgisnacht', Herder can see nothing right in his own age. He sees only evil, not good. To be sure he postulates the formation of a supreme international arbitration court of all the rulers of Europe, in order to prevent wars; he comes out strongly on the side of freedom of thought; but this level is not sustained.

He wrote chiefly in enmity of Goethe and Schiller, and what he regarded as their subordination of all things to aesthetic standards. He ostentatiously ignored their existence, and himself proceeded to contribute theoretical and practical works intended to outdo their achievement. In the drama he required an ethical content that would illustrate the eternal law of Nemesis, after the Greek example, and his ultimate conclusions approximated to Lessing's interpretation of Aristotle's *katharsis*. Among his dramatic efforts were *Admetus' Haus* and an *Entfesselter Prometheus*, which latter was written in opposition to August Wilhelm Schlegel's *Ion* and was later set to music by Liszt. His theory of the epic, as of the drama, was similarly designed to exclude Goethe from the field. It led to major results for Herder himself. Some years earlier, in 1795, before the breach with the Classical writers, he had summed up, in Schiller's *Horen*, the results of his study of Ossian, Homer, and primitive poetry, and had arrived, like Friedrich August Wolf, whom he anticipated, at the theory of the lyrical or ballad origin of the epic. He had formed the opinion that the specific function of the epic was to represent what is heroic or noble in human behaviour and to illustrate the workings of the divine in earthly affairs. In his *Cid*, which is quite the finest single jewel of Herder's whole work, he put this theory into practice. The sources of the *Cid* were Sepúlveda's collection of Spanish ballads and the French prose version contained in the well-known *Bibliothèque universelle des romans*. On the one hand, Herder followed what he imagined to be the usual procedure in epic composition. He assumed the same attitude to his material as he believed Macpherson, in particular, or indeed any epic writer, adopted towards *his*, freely altering and combining, in order to produce a continuous whole. On the other hand, he strove to incorporate the purest and highest qualities of humanity in his work. The *Cid* is not a mere reproduction. It is an original creation of Herder's, and it has enjoyed real popular success ever since its publication.

Elsewhere in the *Adrastea*, Herder wrote of nature-philosophy in the same manner as Schelling, though without his metaphysics. He set up a fantastic poetic theory of light in silent opposition to Goethe's optical studies. He continued Lessing's ideas on freemasonry. He wrote foreshadowing the music-drama of Wagner. There seemed no end to his efforts or his plans. He announced, in particular, a new collection of folksongs, which was to be arranged according to nationalities and was to serve the cause of *Humanität* more expressly than the earlier anthology had done. The work was to be, as he put it,

'eine lebendige Stimme der Völker, ja der Menschheit selbst, wie sie in allerlei Zuständen sich mild und grausam, fröhlich und traurig, scherzhaft und ernst hie und da hören ließ, allenthalben für uns belehrend.'[1]

Herder did not live to carry out his plan, but his description 'Stimme der Völker', owing to the excessive enthusiasm of an adoring editor, Georg Müller, has been remembered and misapplied to the anthology of 1778–9.

Herder had returned to his first love once again. Folk-poetry was his eternal consolation. That which he proclaimed as the key to fresh achievements in literature was now more than ever before a refuge from the insufficiencies of the present. In it he could lose himself utterly. To the end Herder was a preacher and teacher, only now without the prospects of thirty years before. He ended as a voice crying in the wilderness, but the voice was that of a disappointed prophet.

---

[1] XXIV. 266; 'A living voice of the nations, indeed of mankind itself, as it was heard in all conditions and in all places, a voice that is gentle and cruel, happy and sad, merry and serious, everywhere instructive for us.'

H

CHAPTER IX

FORTUNES AND MISFORTUNES

IT was Herder's tragedy that the literary movement he set on foot developed in its own way and not in his. He was not born to command, but to inspire and to suggest. He was before all else a teacher, and self-effacement, the teacher's final reward and the measure of his success, was his lot, though no one bore it more grudgingly. His thoughts, lavished in all directions, so original and so stimulating, quickly became the whole world's property; to their author was left only the mortifying spectacle of watching others take possession of the kingdom to which he had pointed the way, and seeing them rule it in a manner that was not his. So life ended in bitter aloofness and baffled desolation. He was no more than the oracle of a small circle of devoted admirers. Yet few writers of a past age have remained so refreshing and so invigorating. The reader of to-day pauses time and again at the most modern of ideas. There is hardly a branch of human culture which is not indebted to him, directly or indirectly, though few are aware of their ultimate obligation. Hardly any other writer surveyed the whole extent of human effort with so profound a sympathy and so elevated an ideal. Few have suffered so much from the lack of sustained clarity and precision in their writing, and from the mingling of triteness with originality. It was not in Herder's nature that it should have been otherwise.

All who knew Herder personally found him more than usually inspiring. Youth was particularly attracted. After Goethe in those early Strassburg days, Jean Paul, Hölderlin, Georg Müller, Novalis, Ritter, G. H. Schubert, not to mention British visitors such as Crabb Robinson, sought and enjoyed his society. His personal influence was immense. The young people of Riga regarded him as 'their Christ'. He preached 'like a god', and won a bride with a sermon. Goethe has recorded the effect of his meetings with him at Strassburg, Jean Paul has given us revealing impressions, especially in the important passage at the end of the *Vorschule der Ästhetik*, and Georg Müller has devoted a whole book to his life in Herder's house, whither he walked all the way from Göttingen, attracted by the fame of the great man. So vast and irresistible was his influence that one is bound to ask whether it did not completely engulf his pupils. Is there not a

HERDER

Portrait ascribed to Anton Graff

note in Goethe's report, for instance, that he was so absorbed, even overawed, as to be utterly lost and confused?

Without Herder it would be difficult to realize what would have happened to the course of German literature. Almost at a blow he shattered the *Aufklärung* and in a few short years saw German letters marching forward on fresh lines. A decade after the *Fragmente* the *Sturm und Drang* was fully established; another decade saw Goethe's visit to Italy and Schiller's transition to Classicism; still another witnessed the birth of Romanticism. The speed of progress was tremendous. The meeting with Goethe was the decisive event in modern German literature, for it turned the young beginner from traditionally Rationalist attempts to new modes in which his genius learned to fulfil itself. Not only Goethe's poetic evolution, but Bürger's balladry, the native simplicity of Claudius and the other poets of the *Hainbund*, and the work of those who came in the wake of *Götz von Berlichingen* and *Werther*, all are indebted to Herder as their fountain-head. The whole doctrine of spontaneity and naturalness—the seeking after native beginnings, the cult of genius, the Faustian theory of striving, the sombre bursting-forth of the demonic forces of individuality, the violent substitution of feeling for reason, patriotism, the new religious background, the desire for direct and popular peech, the discovery of the real value of Shakespeare and the folksong, of Homer and the Bible, and, above all, the dawning of the historical sense—all this derives from those dark days in Strassburg. Thanks to Herder, German literature was never again to be the pupil of France or of any other country. He began a revolution that was to have no end. The liberation brought immense, unimagined possibilities in its train. But secure moorings had first to be found, and the search for them had many phases, each defective in some degree and in time discarded. Herder made German literature self-conscious. He drove it into ever deeper probings into its own nature, in an effort to find stability. Introspection led to titanism, to despair, to morbid subjectivity, to arrogant self-sufficiency, then and now. The crisis is still unsolved.

Classicism was the first solution attempted. Here again Herder provided the basis. No understanding of it is complete without a careful reading of his works. Its thought-content was gathered together in him. It was largely through personal intercourse with Goethe that his influence was exerted. The doctrines of the *Ideen* and their offshoots—poured into Goethe's receptive ears—underlie the mature production of this poet to the end of his life. The teachings of the completed *Faust*, and of the completed *Wilhelm Meister*; the orientalism of the *Divan*, not to speak of the scientific studies in which Goethe attempted to understand man's position in his background, clearly owe much to Herder's inspiration. Herder's *Humanität*, to which Goethe paid eloquent tribute in *Die Geheimnisse* and the *Maskenzug* of 1818, covers Weimar Classicism in its entirety. Nor must we forget the effect exerted by his essay on 'Nemesis' upon Schiller's *Über Anmut und Würde* and the growth of those aesthetic doctrines that were later to cause his supercession by Schiller in Goethe's heart.

On the Romantic writers, too, the personal influence of Herder was most marked, though his influence was not merely a personal one. Indeed, it is not too much to say that the whole of the Romantic movement in Germany is Herder's intellectual legacy. He was really just as much a leader at the end of the eighteenth century as he had been thirty years before, only his leadership was not fully acknowledged. The teachings of the *Sturm und Drang* as well as of *Humanität*, among which the young Romanticists grew to manhood, cannot be stressed too much. The variety of their modes of application and radiation soon became apparent in an unexpected degree in the writings of the new generation. The universality of his works gave them a wide appeal. Timely developments and re-presentations of his earlier views, such as we find in the explanatory essays of his *Terpsichore* or in the *Zerstreute Blätter* or *Humanitätsbriefe* played a significant part.

Many of the younger men were conscious of their debt. Others were not, and felt themselves to be the followers of Goethe. Of them all, Jean Paul stood closest to Herder, who admired his wit and fancy and found an ally in him against Kant and Fichte. Herder lifted him as if by magic into the realms of poetry and opened his eyes to the vast benevolence of God in the universe, and in the last days of his life Jean Paul had the *Ideen* read to him. His judgement (which De Quincey quoted) is that of a devoted disciple—

'War Er kein Dichter, . . . so war Er blos etwas Besseres, nämlich ein Gedicht, ein indisch-griechisches Epos, von irgend einem reinsten Gott gemacht. . . . Aber wie soll ichs auseinander setzen, da in der schönen Seele, eben wie in einem Gedichte, alles zusammenfloß und das Gute, das Wahre, das Schöne, eine unteilbare Dreieinigkeit war?—Griechenland war Ihm das Höchste, und wie allgemein auch Sein episch-kosmopolitischer Geschmack lobte und anerkannte—sogar Seines Hamanns Stil—, so hing

Er doch, zumal im Alter, wie ein vielgereister Odysseus nach der Rückkehr aus allen Blüten-Ländern, an der griechischen Heimat am innigsten.'[1]

We are told that his eyes filled with tears when he spoke Herder's name. Hölderlin, with his friends Hegel and Schelling, absorbed, in Tübingen, Herder's philosophy of history and his demands for a cultural revival. In 1796 Hölderlin planned a periodical significantly called *Iduna*, the goddess of rejuvenation, after the title of Herder's dialogue which Schiller had so reluctantly published in the *Horen*. He reproduced Herder's apotheosis of Greek civilization in a more profound poetic form in his *Hyperion*, in which novel the figure of Adamas, who sets off to Asia to discover a people of rare excellence, may well represent Herder. Hölderlin was fully acquainted with the doctrine of *Volksgeist*; he shared Herder's view of language as the educator of mankind and followed in his wake by regarding Nemesis as a metamorphosis of the goddess of love. The oneness of man, nature, and the divine was fundamental to his work. He regarded himself as being in the service of *Humanität*, despite Schelling's warning of the discredit in which this term stood. His poetry fed upon the doctrine of 'Stirb und werde' contained in the essay 'Tithon und Aurora' and continued Herder's application of it to the individual and to the nation. Throughout his creative life he held before him the ideal of a higher order of human existence, of beauty and harmony and greatness, built upon a poetic consciousness of nature and a following out of her teachings.

'Unendlich schöner', Herder had said, 'ist das Werk, der Natur nachzugehen und auf ihre Zeiten zu merken, Kräfte zu wecken, woirgend sie schlummern, Gedanken, Tätigkeit, Erfindung, Lust und Liebe zu befördern, in welchem Feld nützlicher Beschäftigungen es auch sein möge. Endlich kommt die Notwendigkeit, und treibt mit einem eisernen Zepter; wer der Vernunft und Billigkeit dient, kommt der Notwendigkeit zuvor, und dar mit Oberons Lilienstabe nur winken, so sprießen hier statt der verwelkten neue Blumen. . . .'[2]

Hölderlin was not alone in agreeing with this.

[1] *Sämtliche Werke*, I. xi, Weimar, 1935, 429-30; 'If he was not a poet, . . . he was something better, namely a poem, a Graeco-Hindu epic, written by the purest of gods. . . . But how am I to explain it, since in his soul, as in a poem, all things met together, and the good, the true, and the beautiful formed an indivisible trinity? Greece was the highest thing of all in his eyes, and however universal were the praise and recognition that his epic, cosmopolitan taste, and even his Hamannesque style vouchsafed, he nevertheless clung, especially in his old age, to his Greek homeland most fondly, like a much-travelled Odysseus returning from all the lotus-lands.'
[2] XVI. 120; 'It is infinitely more beautiful to follow nature and to heed her seasons, to awaken strength wherever it may be slumbering, to encourage thought, activity, invention, pleasure, and love in whatever field of useful occupation they are to be found. In the end necessity comes,

The brothers Schlegel, in method and material, followed Herder's lead. Friedrich was consciously inspired by the challenge of the *Fragmente*, and his work *Über das Studium der griechischen Poesie* was the answer to Herder's cry for a 'Winckelmann of Greek literature'. His Oriental studies go back directly to Herder's pioneer work, as does the demand for a new mythology which he held in common with other Romanticists. His critical survey of literature in the important Vienna lectures of 1812 is a development of the Herderian tradition. His brother August Wilhelm, despite his condemnation of the *Ideen* as containing neither ideas, nor philosophy, nor history, nor humanity, was an apt, even admiring pupil, from the early essay on Dante to the end of his life. His critical technique is entirely in Herder's spirit. He followed his master in the field of translation, in his interest in medieval and foreign literatures, and in his views on the plastic arts, while his Berlin and Vienna lectures gave a survey, such as Herder had sketched so frequently, of the whole course of world-literature. As has been seen, the evolution of Herder's results into the Schlegelian antithesis of Classic and Romantic was an easy one. Yet August Wilhelm's hostility in his middle period was a great disservice to Herder's reputation, since it coloured the instruction he gave to Mme de Staël on German literature.

Novalis stood particularly close to Herder and visited him often. His ideas on a new mythology, his visions of an after-life, his medievalism, his Marian cult, his dreams of a renewal of human civilization on a higher plane, are all traceable to sources in Herder's writings. Wackenroder's interest in German medieval and sixteenth-century poetry came through his teacher Koch, a philological follower of Herder; and Wackenroder passed on his interest to Tieck, his intellectual executor, whose *Minnelieder* attracted Jakob Grimm to Middle High German spheres, and who became an associate of Novalis at a decisive period. Tieck's own English and Spanish studies do not seem to have been directly inspired by Herder, but there can be no doubt of the value of the preparatory work of the latter for their developments later on. Indeed, taken all in all, the philological achievements of Romanticism, leading to the researches of the Grimms, Bopp, and others, grew directly from Herder's pioneer work. His philosophy of language was taken over by Wilhelm von Humboldt, his folksong collection was a standing source of inspiration to all and led to *Des Knaben Wunderhorn*, as well as to the parallel

and moves with an iron sceptre; he who serves reason and equity, anticipates necessity and need only make a sign with Oberon's lily-wand for new flowers to spring forth to take the place of withered ones. . . .'

efforts in allied fields, such as the *Teutsche Volksbücher* of Görres and the *Märchen* of the brothers Grimm. Lachmann's theory of the lyrical origin of the *Nibelungenlied* goes back, through August Wilhelm Schlegel's Berlin lectures and Wolf's view of Homeric origins, to Herder's thoughts on the ballad beginnings of all epic, set forth in the Ossian-essay of 1773. And Lachmann's theory has had vast repercussions, both in Germany and elsewhere.

The Romantic theologian Schleiermacher adopted Herder's differentiation between dogma and faith. Historiography, as represented by Niebuhr and later by Ranke, and expounded by Wilhelm von Humboldt, owed him a great debt, as did the historical law school of Savigny and Hugo. Upon the political Romanticism of the younger groups Herder's influence was incalculable, though their patriotism was intensified by the French military occupation that he was not to know, and untempered by the gentle serenity that marks his idealism. Fichte and Arndt were under a great obligation to him in their stress upon the mother-tongue as being the basic factor in nationality; Stein found him to be one of his favourite authors, while his doctrine of mutual co-operation was influential in the establishment of the *Tugendbund*. No wonder that in 1812 Wilhelm Grimm could say that his spirit still lived actively and effectively among the Germans!

In the sphere of philosophy, Schelling acknowledged his dependence upon Herder in the very title of his *Ideen zu einer Philosophie der Natur*, for his whole conception of nature was indebted to those other *Ideen* and to *Gott*. His youthful dissertation on the Book of Genesis reflected the *Älteste Urkunde*, while his studies of mythology also went back to Herder's findings. Hegel, too, developed much of Herder's material in his philosophy of history. Indeed, *Gott*, not only by bringing Spinoza into the foreground of philosophical thought and thus continuing what Jacobi had started, but also by adapting and re-casting that thinker's doctrines, exerted a far greater influence than is commonly supposed. The Neo-Spinozism of Herder and Goethe, which quickly became part of the intellectual stock of the times— and not so much Spinoza himself—underlies much of subsequent German philosophy. Kant is not its only major starting-point. The monistic conception of the universe and the dynamic view of nature as the living manifestation of the divine spirit are fundamental to Schelling and Hegel. Alexander von Humboldt's *Cosmos* continues the thought of the *Ideen*, while at a later date Lotze's *Mikrokosmos* repeated Herder's effort in the light of modern circumstances. Thus, all modern philosophy of history, that most German of all sciences, is unthinkable without Herder. In a contiguous field, the work of Ratzel, the geographer, is in the Herderian tradition. Houston Stewart Chamberlain twisted Herder's view of the regenerating effect of the invasion of the Roman Empire by the Teutonic tribes into what we now know as the 'Nordic myth', while Hegel's state-philosophy emerged from his idea of 'organic' group development. These aberrations came from over-emphasis upon single aspects of Herder's work. The whole kernel of his philosophy, while it studies the individual in relationship to his background, refuses to allow him to be swallowed up within it and to be merely the passive expression of it, whether it be nation or religion or race or class. These things exist for man, not man for them.[1]

Scherer, with good reason, described the German Romantic move-ment as 'that group of German writers which developed and made the most of Herder's suggestions'.[2] His appeal was immense. His vitalistic conception of nature, his probings into the deepest recesses of her activity, his stress upon the emotional, instinctive, sub-con-scious elements in human life opened up new vistas for the younger generation. In the manner in which he set poetry, as the expression of man's profoundest creative powers, in the forefront of all things and emphasized before all else those factors that produce poetry, Herder was responsible for that 'poetization' of all life which was the ambition of the Romanticists, that 'thinking in sweet sounds', that discovery in poetry of a fuller expression of beauty and truth and goodness than is possible in any other mode of human utterance, that recasting of all life into the mould of myth and magic, fantasy and mysticism, legend and fairy-tale. Poetry as the mother-tongue of the race and poetry as the greatest educating agent were twin themes both in Herder and in Romanticism. It was not for nothing that his *Terpsichore* and its accompanying essays found such favour with August Wilhelm Schlegel, or his *Paramythien*, those original alle-gorical applications of Greek myth, with Novalis. Finally, his con-ception of the *Volk*, the people, as a vast creative unit was a powerful source of inspiration to the new movement. Just as he had once shown Goethe that poetry was a universal gift, so now, reacting

[1] Cf. the very Herderian essay by the late Sir Arthur Keith, *The Place of Prejudice in Modern Civilization*, Aberdeen University Rectorial Address, London, 1931, which incidentally quotes Adam Smith and Thomas Reid in support of the thesis that 'the place of prejudice [i.e. the instincts, desires, and other devices of the human heart] in our modern civilization should be that of servant, not of master' (p.53); 'prejudice' is the indispensable machinery of nature for the purpose of evolution.

[2] *Kleine Schriften*, II, Berlin, 1893, 238.

against the aristocratic exclusiveness of Weimar Classicism, he transmitted the same doctrine to the poets of the new school, directing them to the people in all its manifestations—in language, history, legend, song, music, tradition—as a never-failing source, and to regard themselves as its spokesmen. This is quite apart from his nationalism. Poetry and life were never before brought so closely together. The whole range of literature was widened; poetry was indeed henceforth infinitely 'progressive and universal'.

In the small but steady stream of interest shown in German literature in England at the end of the eighteenth century, Herder seems to have played little more than a minor rôle. He had certainly the great advantage of finding a meritorious translator for his *Ideen*, but few positive repercussions accrued. Knowledge of him was limited, and in any case he counted mainly as a theologian and philosopher and as such appealed to specialized readers only. This may be the reason why he escaped the attacks levelled against Goethe and Schiller that accompanied their introduction into this country. As early as 1776 Herder's *Ursprung der Sprache* had been summed up in the *Monthly Review*, and again in 1784; in this latter year the same journal recommended *Vom Geist der Ebräischen Poesie*, which it proceeded to study in detail in a remarkable review in 1789. The latter work was partially translated in 1801, and the translation afforded yet another opportunity for the *Monthly* to praise Herder. The first work of his, however, to be rendered into English was the essay on Ulrich von Hutten in 1789, and the translator Aufrère wrongly ascribed it to Goethe. The *Monthly Review* discussed it, subsequently reviewing *Gott* in 1792, 'Über Liebe und Selbstheit' in 1793, and the *Zerstreute Blätter* in 1796. The *British Critic* noticed 'Von Gottes Sohn' (in the *Christliche Schriften*) in 1798 and the *Metakritik* in 1800, while the *Monthly Magazine*, which had mentioned Herder in 1798, analysed the *Kalligone* in 1801. But the greatest event of all was the appearance in 1800 of T. Churchill's excellent translation of the *Ideen* (*Outlines of a Philosophy of the History of Man*, London, Johnson; second edition 1803). This was recommended by the *Critical Review*, which praised Herder's 'purest religion and warmest benevolence', rejected by the *British Critic* with a 'feeling of despair of ever meeting with satisfaction from the fashionable philosophy or metaphysics of Germany', and surveyed with some fairness by the *Monthly*. About the same time, small beginnings were made in Scotland, in the shape of efforts by a young contributor to the *Edinburgh Review*, a certain James Mac-

Donald, who knew Herder and circulated manuscript translations of parts of the *Christliche Schriften* among acquaintances, but no roots appear to have been struck. The indefatigable William Taylor of Norwich discussed Herder from time to time, illustrating his numerous reviews with miscellaneous translations, from the Shakespeare-essay, the *Volkslieder*, and the *Zerstreute Blätter*; he summed up his remarks in his *Historic Survey of German Poetry* (1828-30). His knowledge was incomplete and superficial, but his designation of Herder as the 'Plato of the Christian world' has remained current. Thanks to Taylor and Churchill, Herder was known at the turn of the century to small and interested circles as a man of vast learning and great imagination, a notable preacher and a venerable character, full of noble idealism and amplitude of outlook.

Meantime, Matthew Gregory Lewis drew on the *Volkslieder* for ballads included in his *Monk* and his *Tales of Wonder*, and may indeed have met Herder when he visited Weimar in 1792-3. When Lewis' work became known in France, these ballads helped to foster the interest of French Romanticism in folklore. Henry Crabb Robinson found Herder, next to Goethe, to be the one who attracted him most in Weimar, when he saw him in 1801-3; he spoke of English literature with him, lent him the *Lyrical Ballads* and defended Gray and Collins. He remembered Herder with affection and was fascinated by him more than by any other of the Weimarians, on account of the warmth and elevation of his sentiments. An article by him on Herder was, however, returned by the *Monthly Review* in 1803 because of lack of public interest. In contrast to Robinson, Coleridge was openly hostile, as might be expected from an enthusiastic follower of Kant. His marginalia are savagely abusive, culminating in the final judgement 'coxcomb'. Herder's friend Heyne may have spoken of him to Coleridge in Göttingen; soon after the latter's return to England in 1799 he declared his desire to know the *Ideen* and suggests that Southey should borrow a copy from Taylor. He certainly knew the major works of Herder, and there are many points of affinity between the two men, e.g. in their attitude to the French drama, their conception of the divine agency of poetry, and the historical approach to Shakespeare. The *Kalligone* and *Metakritik* were condemned as 'disgusting' and Kant's critique of the *Ideen* was praised as a model review. Though he attacked Herder for his inconsistencies, his lack of logic and his uncertain faith, Coleridge was not above borrowing material from him for his lectures, without acknowledgement.

De Quincey's essay of 1823, defending Herder against Coleridge, was a step forward, though his vision is scarcely more than super-ficial, being based on Jean Paul, Caroline Herder's *Erinnerungen*, and possibly Crabb Robinson. He regarded Herder as the German Coleridge, and could not refrain from saying that he would have been the better of a little opium. Carlyle deplored Taylor's inade-quacy, but he deplored Herder's anti-Kantian attitude, too. He sided with Fichte, an enemy of Herder, second only to Kant. Thus, little progress was made, in spite of Carlyle's quotation of Jean Paul's opinion and his discussion of Goethe's debt to Herder in Strassburg; he objected to the determinism of the *Ideen*, declaring that the book would be reckoned atheistical, 'if Herder were not known as a devout man and clerk'.[1] In 1817 *Blackwood's Magazine* published a translation of 'Elvershöh.' *A Brief Commentary on the Revelation of St. John* appeared in 1821, two *Paramythien* in 1826, and a *Treatise upon the Origin of Language* in 1827, which the translator hoped would con-tribute 'to more amalgamation between the Germans and the English . . . [and] render peculiar national qualities more intelligible'. The *Cid* followed in 1828, while in 1829 an anonymous poem to Herder's memory was printed in the *Gentleman's Magazine*. But the fact remained, England still made very little of Herder.

The *Volkslieder* suggested to Felicia Hemans the idea of her *Lays of Many Lands*, while her *Songs of the Cid* were also indebted to Herder. It was perhaps she who drew Scott's attention to Herder's collection, though he on his part did little more than note that it contained few native specimens. Mrs. Sarah Austin's *Characteristics of Goethe* (1833) revealed fragmentary knowledge. F. B. Hawkins' *Germany and the Spirit of her History, Literature and Social Conditions* (1838) gives a brief account, as do the writings of J. Gostwick, while four *Paramythien* were translated in the *Fables and Parables* of 1845. G. H. Lewes' *Life of Goethe* (1855) is a real landmark which fixes the whole line of approach until the time of R. Flint (*Philosophy of History in France and Germany*, 1874) and H. W. Nevinson (*A Sketch of Herder and his Times*, 1884). Since this last, no independent study of Herder has appeared until F. McEachran's *Life and Philosophy of Herder* in 1939. Herder continued to be studied mainly in his relation to Goethe, and especially, indeed almost exclusively, to the young Goethe; so that all attention came to be devoted to the early works of Herder. Recently, Eric Linklater[2] has paid tribute to Herder's influence on the growth of his Scottish (or Orcadian) nationalism and on the

---

[1] *Two Notebooks*, 72-3; cf. C. F. Harrold, *Carlyle and German Thought*, Yale, 1934, 157.
[2] In *The Man on My Back*, London, 1941, 227-8.

genesis of his novel, *The Men of Ness*, at the same time emphasizing
the presence of the Herderian spirit in the writings of Douglas Hyde,
Lady Gregory, and their followers.

The reception of Herder in America reflects largely the same
features as his reception in England. English criticisms, starting with
Taylor's, were reproduced. George Bancroft drew a biographical
portrait, J. Marsh translated *Vom Geist der Ebräischen Poesie* in 1833,
while Longfellow's *Poets and Poetry of Europe* (1845) praised Herder
and gave translations of four poems. The *Prose Writers of Germany*
(1848), by F. H. Hedge, gave 'Über Liebe und Selbstheit', 'Über die
Seelenwanderung', and 'Tithon und Aurora', and H. C. Fish's *History
and Repository of Pulpit Eloquence* (1857) contains a sermon of Herder's.
Karl Hillebrand's articles in the *North American Review* (1872-3) were
well-informed and most appreciative. An uncommonly useful translation of *Gott*, with an informative introduction and notes, has
recently been published by F. H. Burkhardt (New York, 1940). It
well maintains the high standard of American research on Herder.

In France, as in England and America, Herder was not appreciated
until late in the nineteenth century, and his influence was limited.
It is true that his *Fragmente* were mentioned as early as 1767 by the
Journal Encyclopédique, and this review and the *Gazette des Deux Ponts*
continued to pay him attention. His works seem nearly all to have
been noticed soon after their publication. The *Ursachen des gesunknen
Geschmacks* touched the French *amour-propre*; the *Ursprung der Sprache*
occasioned some discussion; but the *Älteste Urkunde*, *An Prediger*, and
the *Plastik* seem to have escaped notice, until they emerged in the
wake of Lavater. Small translations began to appear, and by the end
of his life Herder was sufficiently famous to miss election to the
Institut only by a small margin on the occasion when Niebuhr
defeated him. His dispute with Kant made him appear to be of the
same rank as the philosopher. The liberalism of his theology attracted
the Protestants and did not displease the Catholics; he seems to have
been regarded as the 'German Fénelon'. Obituary notices were very
favourable.

Mme de Staël's *De l'Allemagne* is not so effective concerning Herder
as it might have been; he was on his deathbed when that redoubtable
lady arrived in Weimar and was thus spared a garrulous inquisition.
August Wilhelm Schlegel was her main informant on Herder, and
he was unsympathetic to him in these years. Nor had the Coppet
circle generally an interest in him. Her first impressions had been

favourable, but she could scarcely resist the hostility of those around her. Her account is disappointingly superficial and surprisingly ignorant. And Herder was one of those who had attracted her to Weimar! Mme de Krüdener was a fervent reader of the *Ideen*. Bonstetten had recourse to Herder in his *Etudes de l'Homme*. Sismondi judged Germany in the same way as Mme de Staël did, depending upon the views of Schlegel. He knew the *Cid*, thought that Herder had studied all the Spanish originals and had himself collected ballads of the Cid, and that his poem was superior to the Spanish cycles, since he had chosen, with taste and discrimination, the best from among his sources. He translated many of Herder's *Cid* ballads as if they were genuine and included them in his famous work *De la Littérature du Midi de l'Europe* (1813). Only later did Sismondi discover his mistake. Creuzé de Lesser discovered the Cid stories of the *Bibliothèque universelle des romans*, Herder's main source, and in 1806 conceived the idea of imitating them; his version appeared in 1814. He did not know Herder's work until his own was nearly finished, and then only in Sismondi's partial translation. He had Escobar's collection at hand, but he did not think of comparing Herder's *Cid* with it. He was wilfully blind. He even spoke of a Cid *edition* by Herder. Benjamin Constant, an earnest student of the *Ideen*, described Herder's works, with ambiguous reverence, as 'un lit bien chaud et bien doux, où l'on rêve agréablement', and found his views of the beginnings of Christianity to be the exact opposite of those stated in 'l'absurde ouvrage de Chateaubriand'. He acquired new facts from Herder in support of his general ideas, but he found him vague and lacking in positive data. Herder aided his evolution, and left his mark especially upon *De la Religion* (1825).

By this time, most informed people knew a little about Herder. Napoleon's physician Barthez translated a fragment of the *Ideen*, Michel Berr admired and thought of translating the *Ebräische Poesie*, Degérando gave the first complete survey in French of Herder's life and work in his obituary notice of 1804, and followed this with accounts in the *Biographie Universelle* (1857) and the *Histoire de la Philosophie Moderne* (1858). He compared him to Fénelon. Ballanche's *Du Sentiment* (1801) quoted Herder, but here, as elsewhere, it was a case of supporting or assisting the development of existing ideas rather than of transmitting new ones. Guizot read Herder in Stapfer's library and admired the section in the *Ideen* dealing with the Romans. But Guizot's history was not the same as Herder's, either in intention or execution, and he owes little to him.

There are some points of affinity, but not of agreement, between Herder and those prophets of reaction, De Maistre and Bonald. Stendhal mentions Herder only to apply the term *niaiserie* to his work; but as this represented his opinion of German thought in any case, no special significance need be inferred. Auguste Comte presents a further instance of Herder as a support and not as an influence. Casual and unimportant references are to be found in France in the years subsequent to *De l'Allemagne*, which note Herder as an orientalist or as a scholar, rather than as a philosopher. Loève-Veimars gave an enthusiastic, if inexact, account of Herder in 1826 in his *Résumé de l'histoire de la littérature allemande*; the *Globe* and the *Bibliothèque Germanique* followed on, speaking of his folksong interests.

By this time, however, the famous translation of the *Ideen* by Edgar Quinet was on the point of appearing (1827-8, reprinted 1834). Quinet knew no German when he decided upon this work and his version was based upon Churchill's version, which a Scottish friend Smith had handed to him in 1824. He saw the original for a fortnight only, when he was in London. Quinet's views are contained in the 'Introduction à la Philosophie de l'Histoire de l'Humanité' (1825), which prefaced his translation of the *Ideen*, and in a highly lyrical 'Essai sur les oeuvres de Herder' (1827). The future author of the *Génie des Religions* and *La Création* was profoundly impressed not only by the *Ideen* but by the *Älteste Urkunde* and *Vom Geist der Ebräischen Poesie*. He well saw, however, that Herder's method, unless inspired by unshakable religious faith, would resolve all theological questions into questions of history and philology. He admired his hero's manner of depicting the influence of physical environment upon mankind, while regretting that he did not sufficiently stress human freedom—and, as he said, 'l'histoire, dans son commencement comme dans sa fin, est le spectacle de la liberté, la protestation du genre humain contre le monde qui l'enchaîne, le triomphe de l'infini sur le fini, l'affranchissement de l'esprit, le règne de l'âme'.[1] This dissatisfaction with Herder provided the basis of his own view of history, and no doubt that of Michelet too. Quinet distinguished sharply between Herder and Vico, discerning that the former paid more attention to physical environment, the latter to man's mind. He found that, notwithstanding his hostility to metaphysics, Herder produced a system which involved a conception of duty more absolute even than that of Kant. Yet, while declaring Herder to be too much of a determinist, Quinet admired him as a friend. 'Jamais, non jamais,

[1] Quinet, *Oeuvres*, II. 366.

il ne m'est arrivé de le quitter sans avoir une idée plus élevée de la mission de l'homme sur la terre: jamais sans croire plus profondément au règne de la justice et de la raison, jamais sans me sentir plus dévoué à la liberté, à mon pays et en tout plus capable d'une bonne action.'[1] Herder was, he complained, almost unknown in France, despite his great influence. To what extent, through Quinet, he helped to give rise to a new undogmatic theology and mythology in French poetry and thought is still to be assessed.

Victor Cousin, who encouraged Quinet, declared the *Ideen*, despite the imprecision of the work, to be the greatest monument that had been raised to the history of progress up to his own day, and lectured upon Herder in 1828. Nevertheless, his enthusiasm did not last and it was Hegel rather than Herder who determined his philosophy of history. Indeed, it becomes clear that many who might have been affected by Herder were attracted by Hegel instead. Quinet sent the introduction to his translation of the *Ideen* to Lamartine, and there are points of affinity—but no more—between the poet and Herder. As is evident, the philosophy of history in France had ample native material on which to base itself. The heritage of Bossuet was still alive, and there is nothing that Lamartine could not have derived from French sources. Herder left his imprint, however, upon the development of the historical method of Michelet, the friend of Quinet; among the echoes is Michelet's use of Herder's essay for his chapter on Ulrich von Hutten, in the *Histoire de France*, while the survey given in the *Bible de l'Humanité* is quite in Herder's manner. Jouffroy's historical outlook was likewise affected, despite his objection that facts bent like grass beneath Herder's feet.

After the *Ideen* there followed Baroness Carlowitz' rendering of the *Ebräische Poesie* in 1845, while Tandel provided a further version of the *Ideen* in 1861-2. Herder's renown in the field of folklore became known too late to be of any material importance in France, but in another direction he found an enthusiastic admirer in Ernest Renan. Renan was delighted by the *Ebräische Poesie* in Baroness Carlowitz' translation, he was attracted by the sections on Rome and the East in the *Ideen*, he praised Herder's interpretation of the *Song of Solomon*, and, though he censured the lack of precision of his *penseur-roi*, he loved his philosophy of *Humanität*, his historico-genetic mode of criticism, and his liberal protestantism. Thanks to Herder, he learned to consider humanity rather than the individual, in dealing with

[1] Quinet, *Oeuvres*, II. 379-80.

moral questions. He believed that Herder was a continuation of the best in French thought.

Here Renan comes near to the explanation of Herder's lack of significance in France and in England. His destiny in these countries emphasizes the fact that he gathered together in himself the main currents of Western thought, so that while he presented something new to Germany, the West did not need him and developed without him. By the middle of the nineteenth century there were so many other parallel sources on which to draw, and it is difficult, if not impossible, to draw lines of demarcation. So the story of Herder's fortunes in France seems to be rather that of an affinity than that of a direct influence. Taine springs to mind at once as a kindred spirit; he read Herder and was in his debt. Pierre Leroux quoted him. Maurice Barrès speaks in terms not unlike his. Jean Jaurès' humane co-ordination of nationalism and internationalism is similar to Herder's, while in another field the figure of Debussy emerges as a kind of musical Herder, anxious to free French music from the German tradition, and to link up with the line of native development that ceased with Rameau. It was France that provided the first major work on Herder and his times with C. Joret's *Herder et la Renaissance littéraire en Allemagne au XVIIIe siècle* (1875).

Quinet's translation of the *Ideen* found its way into the hands of Mazzini. Upon this thinker Herder seems to have had an important influence. He can hardly have been any other than attractive to a student of Bruno and Vico. Mazzini's theory of the progress of humanity, his nationalism, his religious conception that life is governed in accordance with an eternal plan of Providence, and his belief in immortality seem at least to have been decisively coloured by the impact of Herder. 'Humanity' is continually on his lips, even amid his blackest conspiracies, and it meant something very like Herder's *Humanität*, equally comprehensive and equally seductive. Almost everywhere in Mazzini's writings may be found sentiments that forcibly recall Herder—e.g. 'As our true well-being consists in living in accordance with the law of our being, the knowledge and fulfilment of the law of humanity is the sole source of good.' ... 'Humanity can only arrive at the knowledge of its Law of Life, through the free and harmonious development of all its faculties.' ... 'That which is true of each individual with regard to the other individuals forming a part of the society to which he belongs, is equally true of every people with regard to humanity.' ... 'Every people has its special mission, which will co-operate towards the fulfilment of the general mission of humanity. That mission constitutes its nationality. Nationality is sacred.'[1] Even down to the view of the 'moral priesthood' of the poet, the kinship with Herder is evident.

Herder's heritage had its greatest effect further East, in the revival of the Slavs. He himself was keenly interested in these peoples, from the time of that youthful meeting with Schwarz-Erla and his subsequent residence in Livonia. He saw in the Slavonic world new vistas of immense possibilities. He created ideal pictures of Peter the Great, of Catherine, and even of Peter III, as great civilizing agents. He listened to Latvian folksongs, he dreamed of himself as the Reformer of Livonia, a second Luther or Zwingli; and of the Ukraine he wrote that it would become a second Greece. Once the regeneration of Livonia could be accomplished, the light, he fancied, would pass thence to all Central and Southern Russia, and spread from there over all Europe. European civilization was tired, he thought, and new life would come to it from the East, if Russia could be made aware of its mission. The East was for him the land of the future; its unspoilt peoples would develop and lead all Europe. It was for Russia, therefore, and not for Germany that he sketched a national civilization.

The world did not know of these mighty plans at the time, as they were hidden in Herder's travel-diary. Their precipitates, however, in the *Volkslieder* and the *Ideen* were immediately effective. The former did not contain many Slavonic specimens; but the book was a great example to be followed. Herder's view of language and literature as cultural instruments did not escape the notice of his Slav disciples. It was to be proclaimed again later by Friedrich Schlege in Vienna, and materially helped the movement that led ultimately to the destruction of the Austrian Empire. The *Ideen* provided an inspiring doctrine, which was an incredible source of comfort and hope to the Slavs. His belief that each nation has the task of bringing mankind nearer to the goal of *Humanität* meant that each could feel a messianic quality within itself. In his survey Herder takes one nation in each epoch to be the main bearer of the human ideal; each must begin where the other left off. The Teutonic peoples' task had been the overthrow of the Roman Empire; there was now no further need for their warlike qualities, and the future was declared to be in the

[1] *Life and Writings of Joseph Mazzini*, III, London, 1891, 31-3.

I

hands of the tireless, peaceful Slavs, who would bring man nearer to *Humanität* than any other nation had done.

No wonder Herder is proclaimed as the father of the Slav Renaissance! His influence was exerted directly and, later, indirectly through Romanticism. The *Volkslieder* inspired similar collections in Slav territories, where, except in Russia and Poland, which already had poetic traditions resting upon other foundations, they became the bases of the national literatures, elevating the language of the people to a literary level and breaking down the linguistic domination of the Church. The beginnings of political revolution are, therefore, rightly sought in the sphere of philology and literature. The Czechs were affected first and most fundamentally. The philologist Josef Dobrovský (1753-1829), like his master Václav Durych (1735-1802), was inspired by Herder; he reproduced Herder's hopeful prophecies and did immeasureable work in arousing interest in the language and history of the Slavs by his famous history of Czech language and literature. Josef Jungmann (1773-1847) strove to purify the Czech language from teutonisms, supplying their place with formations constructed upon the analogy of Polish and Russian. He was a great admirer of Herder, and, in his spirit, founded the national Renaissance upon the people. He rendered Herder's famous chapter on the Slavs into Czech and began the Bohemian patriotic school. Similarly inspired, the Slovaks Pavel Josef Šafařík (1795-1861) and Jan Kollár (1793-1852), both of whom studied at Jena, published folksongs and re-stated and developed Herder's ideal of *Humanität*, coupled with his nomination of the Slavs as the future leaders of mankind. Šafařík glorified Slav antiquity, as the Grimms glorified German antiquity, Kollár demanded a common Slav literature, and in his fiery patriotic poems called upon all Slavs to unite and fulfil their messianic destiny. Both these men were Pan-Slavs. The Czech František Čelakovský (1799-1852) published collections of folksongs belonging to all the Slav peoples, proclaiming, like his hero Herder, the belief that true nationality dwells in folk-poetry. Previously, Bartholemew Kopitár (1780-1844), the Imperial Librarian in Vienna, who was greatly influenced by Herder, had initiated Jugo-Slav philology, while his follower, the great Vuk Karadžić (1787-1864), in the wake of Goethe and Jakob Grimm, collected Serbian folksongs and founded a new literary language based upon the vernacular. The Croats, too, adopted Vuk Karadžić's language, which meant that ultimately the cultural unity of the Jugo-Slavs would follow. All this work accomplished a literary revolution which was largely to inspire the political one. In Poland, Kasimierz Brodzínski (1791-1835), who loved Herder like a friend, stressed the importance of native traditions in literature. It is well-known that folklore was the starting-point of the work of Mickiewicz, and that he later lectured in Paris on the historic mission of the Slavs. Folksongs of the Cashubians, Serbs, Ruthenians, and others were collected and studied; in the Ukraine, folk-poetry was of the utmost importance for Polish Romanticism. Pushkin, the friend of Mickiewicz, bears marks of this same movement, which swept over all Slav lands. Great stress is laid on folk-poetry in the Russia of to-day. Karamzin introduced Herder into Russia, and Alexander Herzen is among those who show his influence.

The next phase was political. The Bohemian historian František Palacký (1798-1876), President of the Slav Congress of 1848, was deeply indebted to Herder. He saw that a study of history is an effective means of quickening the national spirit, and was impressed by Herder's view that Providence chooses a certain nation from time to time to manifest its purposes. The Slavs (like the Germans) applied this to themselves. Grillparzer, who declared that the Slavs learned all they knew from German sources, wrote his biting epigram in this connexion—'Der Weg der neueren Bildung geht/Von Humanität/Durch Nationalität/Zur Bestialität'[1]—yet in spite of this his *Libussa* foresaw the future of the Slavs. The messianic aspect of the Slav Renaissance found acceptance in Russian Pan-Slavism. Mystic ideals of an Orthodox Christian re-birth under Russian leadership rubbed shoulders with the political demands for the conquest of Constantinople. The proselytizing expansionism of Russian Communism was merely one more metamorphosis of the same thing, and at the present time Pan-Slavism is once again the order of the day.

Upon the shoulders of Kollár and Šafařík and Palacký rose the mighty figure of Thomas Garrigue Masaryk, and any one who wishes to see a modern version of Herder's *Humanitätsideal*, should read the works of that great statesman and philosopher of history, particularly the final chapters of *The Making of a State* (1927). Masaryk was a keen student of Herder, as of all German Classicism, and it was a favourite (if debated) thesis of his that the heritage of Hus and Comenius, the Reformer and the educator-Bishop of the Bohemian Brethren, lived on in Leibniz and then in Herder, who in turn retransmitted it to the Czechs through Dobrovský and Kollár, thus repaying the debt that Germany owed to these Bohemian thinkers.

[1] 'The path of modern culture leads from humanity, through nationality, to bestiality.'

After that came Palacký, Šafařík, Karel Havlíček, and Augustin Smetana. Masaryk's theme is that Hus began that movement to overthrow medieval theocracy which ultimately led to modern democracy and the rise of the humane ideal, while Comenius preached the doctrine of universal Christianization and peace. The idea of *Humanität* is clearly in accord with this and Herder had been an enthusiastic adherent of Comenius, after he had become familiar with him in the 1790's.

Again and again the kinship of Masaryk with Herder emerges in striking fashion. He is a democrat, for 'democracy is the political form of the humane ideal'.[1] His view of poets is that they are 'the creators and wardens of national and political ideals.'[2] He condemns the 'thraldom of habit.' He is hostile to Kant. He seeks to penetrate spiritually into the life of individuals, of nations, and of mankind. He demands reciprocity of national influences, and aims at a harmonious association of nationalities. His view is that the theocratic society of the Middle Ages was overthrown by the Reformation, whose work the French Revolution completed. Nothing could illustrate the affinity better than the following statements: 'It is natural that, as a general rule, nationality should be determined by language, for language is an expression of the national spirit. . . . Conscious fostering of nationality implies therefore a comprehensive policy of culture and education. Literature and art, philosophy and science, legislation and the State, politics and administration, moral, religious and intellectual style, have to be national. . . . The relationship between the nation and mankind, between nationality and internationality, between nationalism and humaneness of feeling is not that mankind as a whole and internationalism and humaneness are something apart from, against, or above the nation and nationality, but that nations are the natural organs of mankind. . . . . Chauvinism, racial or national intolerance, not love of one's own people, is the foe of nations and humanity. Love of one's own nation does not entail non-love of other nations.'[3] Yet how hard it has been to keep the flame pure since Herder set it alight! The responsibility is not his for the errors of misguided followers.

The leaves from Herder's branches fell in many places. Nationalism was his most dynamic and fateful gift to the world. Its repercussions in a country even so far away as Finland were consider-

---

[1] *The Making of a State*, London, 1925, 441.   [2] ibid., 412.   [3] ibid., 390.

able, where the cultivation of the folksong and of Shakespeare under his influence by the Åbo Academy in the late eighteenth century prepared the way for the national revival in the nineteenth, when Elias Lönnrot (1802-84) not only created a Finnish literary language but also published the *Kálevala*, epic lays collected by himself and arranged in a unified whole. There are echoes of Herder's work in the Scandinavian writers Franzén, Schack Staffeldt, Tegnér, and Atterbom. Indeed all Baltic territories show the mark of his activity at Riga. Nor must we overlook the stimulus given to the revival of the Hungarians, stung to action by his remark that they were declining. But more than all these external influences, Herder's position in German thought is of dominating significance. Directly, and again through his spiritual heirs and executors, Goethe and the Romanticists, Germany owes more to him than to any one man between Luther and Bismarck.

Herder is the fountain-head of German nationalism. He began by liberating German literature from its subservience to French and Classical models; he ended by expounding a doctrine that viewed nationalism as an indispensable pillar of all civilization. It mattered little that this doctrine contained contradictions; its effectiveness was independent of them. His intention was throughout to teach the Germans to become conscious of themselves and their powers. In doing so, he directed them to probe into their failings as well. So that, while on the one hand he expounded the theory that is contained in the slogan *ex septentrione lux!*, indicating that the Teutons were conferring a benefit upon mankind by invading the Roman Empire— a belief susceptible of remarkable twists to suit future developments— he also encouraged that self-pity, that envy, yearning, and feeling of inferiority that has resulted from Germany's continual self-analysis and retrospect. His achievement was that he gave the Germans something in which to believe—themselves. This explains why he never struck roots in the self-confident West, and why the East, which needed a belief as much as Germany did, received him so gladly.

His cult of genius has had obvious repercussions in the form of the heroic ideal, so idolatrously romanticized in the political sphere in Germany. His emotionalism has given rise to the idea that reason can be discarded as a major factor in human behaviour. Feeling, how- ever, can teach indiscriminately both the fundamental verities of life and passing convictions of the moment. Ephemeral fancies may be proclaimed as if they are eternal truths. Thus Germany is the land of changing beliefs as well as of fundamental beliefs. Further, the cult of feeling has assisted that aesthetic view of things which, since Winckelmann's day, has played so vital a rôle in Germany, and which has taken precedence over the ethical approach.

At a time when all faith was destroyed by Rationalism and when Kant was demonstrating the limitations of reason itself, Herder provided a religious faith that was to become an indelible factor in all his country's thought, a vague and undogmatic faith in a directing, all-embracing divine spirit, of which the world is the living outward manifestation. This faith is ultimately derived from the heritage of medieval Mysticism, that 'consciousness', as Schleiermacher said, 'of the universal existence of all finite things in the infinite and through the infinite, of all temporal things in the eternal and through the eternal', a consciousness that is by nature a part of the German soul. Even in moments of deepest pessimism this belief has not wavered. The Germans have never been blankly hopeless. Human life may be futile, but it is still part of the divine scheme of things and still has some meaning as such. When all else is shattered, the Germans can still believe, and out-and-out pessimism is impossible. When France was bowing down to the goddess of Reason, the Germans were provided with a faith that could sustain them, even if they could not be quite sure about what life's purpose might be. It is Faust's faith, indefinite and unorthodox. It is Herder's contribution and it has passed into universal currency.

The result was phenomenal and immediate. There can be no mistake about it. But for Herder the modern German *Weltanschauung* would have been based primarily only on Kant, the Kant who combated one-sided empiricism only to replace it with equally one-sided intellectualism. Herder tempered the influence of Kant. He gave to men's minds a basis of faith, upon which Kant's system was destined to be superimposed. He prepared the mental atmosphere of Germany. Kant supervened when the ground was already pre-sown with a different seed. The mark of Herder can, therefore, be traced in all later thought, even though it may be covered over by the heritage of Kantianism. It is not Herder's fault if arrogant intellectualism comes to the fore in later times.

This vague belief in an indistinctly defined divine will inherent in the universe is capable, of course, of application in support of anything, for everything can be declared to be its manifestation and to be in accordance with its governance. It may be used, for instance, to justify submission to the state as the mouthpiece of the divine, as it was in Hegel. But, while apparently reducing all problems to simplicity, it nevertheless creates new problems too, when it is unknowingly applied in part. Its seductive imprecision is at the root of the tragic dilemma that has haunted Germany since the days of the *Sturm und Drang*. Perplexities that are given literary expression in that period are indeed real perplexities that recur again and again in practical spheres. The world in actual fact is felt to be so permeated with evil that the good and pure, in their efforts to obey the divine will, are either destroyed, as Ferdinand and Luise are in *Kabale und Liebe*, or are forced in self-defence into criminal rebellion against the circumstances that surround them, at the cost of losing their moral purity, like Karl Moor in *Die Räuber*, and at the cost of great harm to all in their vicinity. In either event the outcome is tragic. All effort seems foredoomed to disaster. Is renunciation or despair, the Germans ask themselves, to be the everlasting lot of man? Is he for ever to be a 'helpless 'ant on the wheel of fate'? Or is he to struggle against what he knows will be disaster, fully aware of his own helplessness? The choice, it seems, lies thus between abandoning all claim to individual existence and striving and suffering. In either case, there results a feeling of self-pity, of martyrdom. Only the greatest, the outstanding supermen, therefore, can strive and achieve anything positive. The consciousness of the oneness of man and nature and God is, as Werther quickly discovered, a source both of comfort and of sorrow—comfort in the feeling of unity with the infinite, sorrow in the feeling of smallness in face of it. German Mysticism is Janus-headed.

All these factors are present, not only in the literature of Germany, but in its history, in all its thought, in all that rhythmical alternation of self-reproach and self-exhortation, resignation and rebellion, despair and self-assertion. Since happiness is impossible, it is given up as a motive in behaviour, and other motives slip into its place. Behind it all is the German conception of God, transcendentalism framed within immanence, as Herder stated it. When Herder wrote, however, he wrote to reveal the positive side of the picture, the consoling doctrine of *Humanität*. This rosy ideal was his answer to the dilemma of the time. Unfortunately, German thought moved so rapidly that *Humanität* was first absorbed by, and then swallowed up in, the welter of progress that was made. Yet it remains, as full of meaning now as on the day it was promulgated, and, as Masaryk has shown, it is capable, when given greater coherence, of inspiring a modern state. Its weakness lies in its susceptibility to being given a partial application; in the manifold radiations, its central glow is apt to be lost to view. The world has, therefore, not seen it in all its fullness. It is democratic and federationist; its nationalism is not expansionist or arrogant, but co-operative, the friend not the enemy of internationalism; its ideal is that of a community of nation-states all striving, in fertile collaboration, towards ever higher spheres of human achievement.

SELECT BIBLIOGRAPHY

THERE is no complete bibliography of Herder in existence. Students must therefore have recourse to the appropriate section in K. Goedeke's *Grundriß zur Geschichte der deutschen Dichtung*, Vol. IV, i, third edition, Dresden, 1916, supplemented by the *Jahresbericht über die wissenschaftlichen Erscheinungen auf dem Gebiete der neueren deutschen Literatur*, Berlin, 1924 ff. (covering the years since 1921).[1] *The Year's Work in Modern Language Studies*, ten volumes, Cambridge, 1931-40, surveys and lists research published since 1930.

The following bibliography contains in the first section a list of Herder's works and correspondence, indispensable for any scholarly research. The second section covers general biographical works, the third deals with special studies on aspects of Herder's writings and influence. A final section lists works that are of use in viewing Herder in his proper perspective. Some overlapping is inevitable, but it is hoped that this arrangement reduces it to a minimum. Many minor works of ephemeral interest are not recorded, and general histories of German literature, all of which include some account of Herder, are similarly omitted.

I. SOURCES

Herder, J. G., *Sämtliche Werke*, hg. von B. Suphan, 33 vols., Berlin, 1877-1913. This is the standard edition; all references in the text are made to it. The selections published by T. Matthias (5 vols.) in *Meyer's Klassiker-Ausgaben*, Leipzig, Bibliographisches Institut, 1903, and by E. Naumann (15 vols.) in *Bongs Goldene Klassiker-Bibliothek*, Leipzig, 1912, are useful. Immediately prior to the war a new selection, arranged according to subject-matter, was in process of publication by F. Schultz (Herder, *Gesammelte Werke*, Potsdam, 1939 f.). In England a small volume of *Kleinere Aufsätze, I* by Herder was published in 1923 by the Cambridge University Press in a plain-text edition, while in the following year the Oxford University Press issued a scholarly edition of *Von Deutscher Art und Kunst* by E. Purdie. F. H. Burkhardt's translation of *Gott* (*God. Some Conversations*, New York, 1940) contains an excellent introduction.

Herder, Maria Caroline von, *Erinnerungen aus dem Leben J. G. von Herders*, hg. von J. G. Müller, 2 vols., Tübingen, 1820.

Herder, Emil Gottfried von (ed.), *Herders Lebensbild*, 3 vols., Erlangen, 1846.

Düntzer, H., and F. G. von Herder (ed.), *Aus Herders Nachlaß*, 3 vols., Frankfurt a.M., 1856-7.

[1] The period 1914-20 is covered by P. Merker's *Deutsche Literaturgeschichte*, Gotha, 1922.

Düntzer, H., and F. G. von Herder (ed.) *Herders Reise nach Italien. Herders Briefwechsel mit seiner Gattin von August* 1788 *bis Juli* 1789, Gießen, 1859.

Düntzer, H., and F. G. von Herder (ed.) *Von und an Herder,* 3 vols., Leipzig, 1861-2.

Hoffmann, O. (ed.), *Herders Briefwechsel mit Nicolai,* Berlin, 1887.

Hoffmann, O. (ed.), *Herders Briefe an J. G. Hamann,* Berlin, 1889.

'Unbekannte Briefe Herders und seiner Gattin an ihre Darmstädter Verwandten,' *Jahrbuch der Goethe-Gesellschaft,* xxi, 1935.

Schauer, H. (ed.), *Herders Briefwechsel mit Caroline Flachsland,* 2 vols., Schriften der Goethe-Gesellschaft, xxxix, xli, Weimar, 1926-8.

Schauer, H. (ed.), *Herders Dresdener Reise. Zehn Briefe J. G. Herders aus dem Jahre* 1803, Dresden, 1929.

Wagner, K. (ed.), *Herders Briefe an J. H. Merck,* Darmstadt, 1835.

Wagner, K. (ed.), *Briefe von und an J. H. Merck,* Darmstadt, 1835.

Bibliotheca Herderiana, Vimariae, 1804 (which supplements the manuscript 'Meine Bücher, den 21. Jun. 776').

II. GENERAL WORKS

Baechthold, J. (ed.), *Aus dem Herderschen Hause,* Berlin, 1881. Charming reminiscences by J. G. Müller.

Bossert, A., *Un prussien libéré. Herder. Sa vie et son œuvre,* Paris, 1916. A brief survey.

Bürkner, R. *Herder, sein Leben und Wirken,* Berlin, 1904. A useful short study.

Gebhardt, P. von and Hans Schauer, *J. G. Herder. Seine Vorfahren und seine Nachkommen,* Leipzig, 1930.

Haym, R., *Herder,* 2 vols., Berlin, 1880-5. The authoritative biography, full of detailed scholarship and ripe wisdom.

Joret, C., *Herder et la renaissance littéraire en Allemagne au* 18e *siècle,* Paris, 1875. Not exclusively about Herder.

Keller, L., *J. G. Herder, seine Geistesentwicklung, seine Weltanschauung,* Jena, 1911.

Kühnemann, E., *Herders Persönlichkeit in seiner Weltanschauung,* Berlin, 1893.

Kühnemann, E., *Herder,* third edition, Munich, 1927. Kühnemann's two books are quite indispensable, and form excellent companions to Haym's extensive work.

McEachran, F., *The Life and Philosophy of J. G. Herder,* Oxford, 1939.

Muthesius, K., *Herders Familienleben,* Berlin, 1904.

Nevinson, H. W., *A Sketch of Herder and His Times,* London, 1884. A comprehensive study in English.

Rasch, W., *Herder. Sein Leben und Werk im Umriß,* Halle, 1938.

Wiese, B. von, *Herder. Grundzüge seines Weltbildes,* Leipzig, 1939.

III. SPECIAL STUDIES

(a) HERDER'S LITERARY CRITICISM AND AESTHETIC THEORY

Adler, F., *Herder and Klopstock*, Diss. Illinois, 1913.

Aron, E., *Die deutsche Erweckung des Griechentums durch Winckelmann und Herder*, Heidelberg, 1929.

Berger, A. E., *Der junge Herder und Winckelmann*, Halle, 1903.

Betteridge, H. T., 'The Ossianic Poems in Herder's *Volkslieder*', *Modern Language Review*, xxx. 1935.

Blochmann, E., 'Die deutsche Volksdichtungsbewegung in Sturm und Drang und Romantik', *Deutsche Vierteljahrsschrift*, i, 1923.

Bojanowski, H. von, 'Herder über Musik', *Goethe-Jahrbuch*, xxx, 1909.

Burdach, K., 'Faust und Moses', *Sitzungsberichte der kgl. preußischen Akademie der Wissenschaften*, 1912. Contains excellent material on the *Älteste Urkunde* and the *Plastik*.

Gillies, A., *Herder und Ossian*, Berlin, 1933.

Gillies, A., 'Herder and the Preparation of Goethe's Idea of *Weltliteratur*', *Publications of the English Goethe Society*, ix, 1933.

Gillies, A., 'Herder's Essay on Shakespeare: "Das Herz der Untersuchung"', *Modern Language Review*, xxxii, 1937.

Grohmann, W., *Herders nordische Studien*, Diss. Rostock, 1902. Contains useful data.

Günther, H., *Herders Stellung zur Musik*, Leipzig, 1903.

Hagenbring, P., *Herder und die romantischen und nationalen Strömungen in der deutschen Literatur des 18. Jahrhunderts*, Diss. Rostock, 1909.

Hausmann, J. F., 'Der junge Herder und Hamann', *Journal of English and Germanic Philology*, vi, 1907.

Huber, K., 'Herders Begründung der Musikästhetik', *Archiv für Musikforschung*, i. 1936.

Isaacsen, H., *Der junge Herder und Shakespeare*, Berlin, 1930.

Jacoby, G., *Herders und Kants Ästhetik*, Leipzig, 1907.

Kircher, E., 'Volkslied und Volkspoesie in der Sturm- und Drang-Zeit', *Zeitschrift für deutsche Wortforschung*, iv, 1903.

Konrad, G., *Herders Sprachproblem im Zusammenhang der Geistesgeschichte*, Berlin, 1938.

Koschmieder, A., *Herders theoretische Stellung zum Drama*, Stuttgart, 1913.

Küntzel, G., *J. G. Herder zwischen Riga und Bückeburg. Die Ästhetik und Sprachphilosophie der Frühzeit nach ihren existentiellen Motiven*, Diss. Frankfurt, 1936.

Längin, T., *Die Sprache des jungen Herder in ihrem Verhältnis zur Schriftsprache*, Diss. Frieburg, 1891.

Lauchert, F., 'Die Anschauungen Herders über den Ursprung der Sprache', *Euphorion*, i, 1894.

Lutz, E., *Herders Anschauungen vom Wesen des Dichters und der Dichtkunst in der ersten Hälfte seines Schaffens*, Diss. Erlangen, 1925.

Markwardt, B., *Herders Kritische Wälder*, Leipzig, 1925. A comprehensive study.

May, K., *Lessings und Herders kunsttheoretische Gedanken in ihrem Zusammenhang*, Berlin, 1923.

Nufer, W., *Herders Ideen zur Verbindung von Poesie, Musik und Tanz*, Berlin, 1929.

Reinke, J., *Herder als Übersetzer altdeutscher Gedichte*, Diss. Münster, 1902.

Sapir, E., 'Herder's *Ursprung der Sprache*', *Modern Philology*, v, 1907.

Schmitz, R., *Das Problem 'Volkstum und Dichtung' bei Herder*, Berlin, 1937.

Schork, L., *Herders Bekanntschaft mit der englischen Literatur*, Diss. Gießen, 1928.

Springmeyer, H., *Herders Lehre vom Naturschönen*, Jena, 1930.

Stavenhagen, K., *Herder in Riga* (Abhandlungen des Herderinstituts in Riga), Riga, 1925. Contains interesting details.

Sturm, W., *Herders Sprachphilosophie*, Diss. Breslau, 1917.

Treutler, A., *Herders dramatische Dichtungen*, Stuttgart, 1915.

Tronchon, H., 'Goethe, Herder à Strasbourg et Diderot', in *Etudes sur Goethe* (Publications de l'Université de Strasbourg), 1932.

Weber, G., *Herder und das Drama*, Weimar, 1922. A comprehensive study of Herder's dramatic theory and practice.

Wedel, M., *Herder als Kritiker*, Berlin, 1928.

Wolf, H., 'Die Genielehre des jungen Herder', *Deutsche Vierteljahrsschrift* iii, 1925. A valuable article.

(b) HERDER'S PHILOSOPHY AND THEOLOGY

Adam, R., 'Wesen und Grenzen der organischen Geschichtsauffassung bei J. G. Herder', *Historische Zeitschrift*, clv, 1937.

Andress, J. M., *Johann Gottfried Herder as an Educator*, New York, 1916. A useful book.

Auerbach, E., 'Vico und Herder', *Deutsche Vierteljahrsschrift*, x, 1932.

Baumgarten, O., *Herders Lebenswerk und die religiöse Frage der Gegenwart*, Tübingen, 1905. A concise and readable account of Herder's work and its religious implications.

Baumgarten, O., *Herders Anlage und Bildungsgang zum Prediger*, Diss. Halle, 1888.

Berger, F., *Menschenbild und Menschenbildung. Die philosophischpädagogische Anthropologie J. G. Herders*, Stuttgart, 1933. A useful, if difficult, work.

Bran, F. A., *Herder und die deutsche Kulturanschauung*, Berlin, 1932. Very sketchy.

Braun, O., 'Herders Kulturphilosophie', *Zeitschrift für Philosophie und philosophische Kritik*, clxiv-v, 1911-12.

Braun, O., 'Herders Ideen zur Kulturphilosophie auf dem Höhepunkt seines Schaffens', *Historische Zeitschrift*, ci, 1912-13.

Bruntsch, M., *Die Idee der Entwicklung bei Herder*, Diss. Leipzig, 1904.

Bruntsch, M., 'Der Geist von Sturm und Drang in der Pädagogik des jungen Herder', *Pädagogische Studien*, xxv, 1904.

Burckhardt, G. E., *Die Anfänge einer geschichtlichen Fundamentierung der Religionsphilosophie bei Herder*, Diss. Halle, 1908.

Clark, R. T., 'The Noble Savage and the Idea of Tolerance in Herder's *Briefe zu Beförderung der Humanität*', *Journal of English and Germanic Philology*, xxxiii, 1934.

Dieterle, J. A., 'Die Grundgedanken in Herders Schrift *Gott* und ihr Verhältnis zu Spinozas Philosophie', *Theologische Studien und Kritiken*, lxxxvii, 1914.

Doerne, M., *Die Religion in Herders Geschichtsphilosophie*, Leipzig, 1927. An uncommonly useful work.

Ergang, R., *Herder and German Nationalism*, New York, 1931. An extremely informative and thorough account of Herder's nationalism and its influence.

Farinelli, A., *L'umanità di Herder e il concetto della 'razza' nella storia evolutiva dello spirito*, Turin, 1919.

Frank, R., *Herders Frankreich-Erlebnis*, Diss. Hamburg, 1933. Weak.

Gemmingen, O. von, *Vico, Hamann und Herder*, Diss. Munich, 1918.

Genthe, T., *Der Kulturbegriff bei Herder*, Diss. Jena, 1902.

Gillies, A., 'Herder's Approach to the Philosophy of History', *Modern Language Review*, xxxv, 1940.

Gillies, A., 'Herder and Pascal', *Modern Language Review*, xxxvii, 1942.

Goeken, W., *Herder als Deutscher*, Stuttgart, 1926.

Gronau, E., *Herders religiöse Jugendentwicklung*, Diss. Kiel, 1931.

Hatch, I. C., *Der Einfluß Shaftesburys auf Herder*, Berlin, 1901.

Hayes, C. J. H., 'Contributions of Herder to the Doctine of Nationalism', *American Historical Review*, xxxii, 1927.

Hoffart, E., *Herders 'Gott'*, Diss. Erlangen, 1917.

Jacoby, G., 'Herder und Schopenhauer', *Jahrbuch der Schopenhauer-Gesellschaft*, vii, 1918.

Keller, L., *J. G. Herder und die Kultgesellschaften des Humanismus*, Berlin, 1904.

Koch, F., 'Herder und die Mystik', *Blätter für deutsche Philosophie*, 1927-8.

Koeppen, W., *Herders Reisetagebuch vom Jahre 1769*, Diss. Greifswald, 1929.

Kohlschmidt, W., *Herder-Studien*, Berlin, 1929.

Koller, A. H., 'Herder's Conception of Milieu', *Journal of English and Germanic Philology*, xxiii, 1924.

Kronenberg, M., *Herders Philosophie nach ihrem Entwicklungsgang und ihrer historischen Stellung*, Heidelberg, 1889.

Kuhfus, H., *Gott und Welt in Herders 'Ideen'*, Diss. Münster, 1938.

Kühnemann, E., 'Herder, Kant, Goethe', *Logos*, ii, 1912.

Lehmann, R., 'Herders Humanitätsbegriff', *Kant-Studien*, xxiv, 1919.

Lehmann, R., *Die deutschen Klassiker: Herder, Schiller, Goethe*, Leipzig, 1921.

Litt, T., *Herder und Kant als Deuter der geistigen Welt*, Leipzig, 1930.

Loerke, O., 'Herders Weltgebäude', *Neue Rundschau*, 1935. Very readable.

McGiffert, A. C., 'The God of Spinoza as interpreted by Herder', *Hibbert Journal*, iii, 1904–5.

Martin, G., 'Herder als Schüler Kants. Aufsätze und Kolleghefte aus Herders Studienzeit', *Kant-Studien*, xli, 1936.

Meyer-Benfey, H., *Herder und Kant*, Halle, 1904.

Neumann, R., *Herder und der Kampf gegen die Kantischen Irrlehren an der Universität Jena*, Progr. Berlin, 1911. Documented.

Ninck, J., *Die Begründung der Religion bei Herder*, 2. Aufl., Leipzig, 1912.

Nohl, H., 'Johann Gottfried Herder', first published in 1905, now in Nohl's *Pädagogische Aufsätze*, Langensalza, 1929. An exceedingly penetrating essay that is insufficiently known.

Noll, R., 'Herders Verhältnis zur Naturwissenschaft und dem Entwicklungsgedanken', *Archiv für die Geschichte der Philosophie*, xxiv, 1913.

Pascal, R., 'Herder and the Scottish Historical School', *Publications of the English Goethe Society*, xiv, 1939.

Posadzy, L., *Der entwicklungsgeschichtliche Gedanke bei Herder*, Diss. Münster, 1906.

Redeker, M., *Humanität, Volkstum, Christentum in der Erziehung. Wesen und gegenseitiges Verhältnis aus der Gedankenwelt des jungen Herder für die Gegenwart dargestellt*, Berlin, 1934.

Saunders, T. B., 'Herder', *Hibbert Journal*, ii, 1904.

Schaede, E. J., *Herders 'Gott' und ihre Aufnahme bei Goethe*, Berlin, 1934.

Schütze, M., 'The Fundamental Ideas in Herder's Thought', *Modern Philology*, xviii, xix, xxi, 1920–4.

See, H., 'La philosophie de l'histoire de Herder', *Revue de Synthèse Historique*, xlviii, 1929.

Siegel, C., *Herder als Philosoph*, Stuttgart, 1907.

Stadelmann, R., *Der historische Sinn bei Herder*, Halle, 1928. One of the most useful shorter works on Herder of recent years.

Stephan, H., *Herder in Bückeburg*, Tübingen, 1905. Amply repays the closest attention, a leading contribution to Herder studies.

Stephan, H., 'Schleiermacher und Herder', *Zeitschrift für Theologie und Kirche*, 1906.

Strothmann, E. W., 'Das scholastische Erbe im Herderschen "Pantheismus"', *Dichtung und Volkstum*, xxxvii, 1936.

Taylor, I., *Kultur, Aufklärung, Bildung, Humanität und verwandte Begriffe bei Herder*, Diss. Gießen, 1938. Definitions.

Tumarkin, A., *Herder und Kant*, Bern, 1896.

Vogel, A., 'Herders 'Journal meiner Reise von 1769'', Diss. Hamburg, 1928.

Vogt, A., *Umrisse einer Staatslehre bei J. G. Herder*, Stuttgart, 1939.

Vollrath, W., *Die Auseinandersetzung Herders und Spinozas*, Diss. Gießen, 1911.

Ward, H. G., 'Herder and the Gypsies', *Journal of the Gypsy Lore Society*, 1935.

Werner, A., *Herder als Theologe*, Berlin, 1871.

Wielandt, R., *Herders Theorie von der Religion und den religiösen Vorstellungen*, Diss. Hiedelberg, 1903.

Wolfram, A., 'Schiller und Herder', *Euphorion*, xxviii, 1927.

(c) HERDER'S INFLUENCE

Alt, J., *Jean Paul*, Munich, 1925.

Berend, E., *Jean Pauls Persönlichkeit*, Munich and Leipzig, 1913.

Bittner, K., *Herders Geschichtsphilosophie und die Slawen*, Reichenberg, 1929. A most informative study.

Böhm, W., *Hölderlin*, 2 vols., Halle, 1928-30.

Closs, A., 'Wurzeln der Romantik bei Herder', *Modern Language Quarterly*, ii, 1941.

Dunstan, A. C., 'The German Influence on Coleridge', *Modern Language Review*, xvii-xviii, 1922-3.

Ehrenberg, V., *Herders Bedeutung für die Rechtswissenschaft*, Festrede, Göttingen, 1903.

Gillies, A., 'A Scottish Correspondent of Wieland's and the Importation of German into Scotland', *Modern Language Review*, xxx, 1935.

Gillies, A., 'The Macrocosmos-Sign in Goethe's *Faust* and Herder's Mystic Hexagon', *Modern Language Review*, xxxvi, 1941.

Gillies, A., 'Herder's Preparation of Romantic Theory', *Modern Language Review*, xxxix, 1944.

Goebel, L., *Herder und Schleiermachers Reden über die Religion*, Gotha, 1904.

Götz, H., 'War Herder ein Vorgänger Darwins?', *Vierteljahrsschrift für wissenschaftliche Philosophie und Soziologie*, xxvi, 1902.

Harrold, C. F., *Carlyle and German Thought*, Yale, 1934.

Jacoby, G., *Herder als Faust*, Leipzig, 1911. Very useful data, but exaggerated conclusions.

Learned, M. D., 'Herder in England and America', *German-American Annals*, 1904.

Leroux, P., 'La philosophie de l'histoire chez Herder et Humboldt', *Mélanges H. Lichtenberger*, Paris, 1934.

Lichtenstein, E., 'Die Idee der Naturpoesie bei den Brüdern Grimm und ihr Verhältnis zu Herder', *Deutsche Vierteljahrsschrift*, vi, 1928.

Little, C. J., 'Herder and Religious Thought', *Methodist Review*, 1904. Very brief, but pleasant.

Montgomery, M., 'Herder's Influence on the Metrical Version of Hölderlin's *Hyperion*', *Studies in the Age of Goethe*, Oxford, 1931.

Petersen, O., *Herder und Hehn*, Riga, 1931.

Pommier, J., 'L'initiation d'Ernest Renan aux lettres allemandes', *Revue de Littérature Comparée*, xv, 1935.

Quinet, E., *Oeuvres*, 10 vols., Paris, 1857-8, and 17 vols., Paris, 1877-9.

Ruprecht, W. K., 'Felicia Hemans und die englischen Beziehungen zur deutschen Literatur im ersten Drittel des 19. Jahrhunderts', *Anglia*, xlvii, 1924. Contains material on Herder.

Schierenberg, R., *Der politische Herder*, Graz, 1932. Deals with Herder's influence in Slavonic countries.

Schmidt, G., *Herder und August Wilhelm Schlegel*, Diss. Berlin, 1917.

Steig, R., 'Wilhelm Grimm und Herder', *Vierteljahrsschrift für Literaturgeschichte*, iii, 1890.

Stockley, V., *German Literature as Known in England*, 1750-1830, London, 1929.

Tronchon, H., *La Fortune intellectuelle de Herder en France*; and *Bibliographie critique*, Paris, 1920. Full of detailed learning, but deals only with the period before Quinet's translation of the *Ideen*. A survey of the later period is very necessary.

Tronchon, H., 'Herder et Lamartine', *Revue de Littérature Comparée*, i, 1921. A long article with negative conclusions.

Tronchon, H., 'Herder et Henri Amiel', *Revue de Littérature Comparée*, iii, 1923. A very slender contact?

Tronchon, H., *Ernest Renan et l'Etranger*, Paris, 1928.

Tronchon, H., *Romantisme et Préromantisme*, Paris, 1930. Includes essays on 'Histoire et Philosophie de l'Histoire aux alentours de 1830', 'Un romantique en Alsace: Edgar Quinet', 'Romanceros préromantiques'.

Tronchon, H., *Etudes*, Paris, 1935. Includes essays on 'Un écho de Pascal outre-Rhin' and 'Herder et Victor Cousin'.

Tronchon, H., *Allemagne—France—Angleterre. Le jeune Edgar Quinet*, Paris, 1937. Mainly an account of the influence of Herder in England and America, and only secondarily about Quinet.

Unger, R., *Herder, Novalis und Kleist. Studien über die Entwicklung des Todesproblems in Denken und Dichten vom Sturm und Drang zur Romantik*, Frankfurt a.M., 1922. A very penetrating work.

Wirth, J., 'Jean Paul und Herder', *Jean-Paul-Blätter*, xii, 1937.

IV. GENERAL WORKS

Adams, H. P., *Life and Writings of Giambattista Vico*, London, 1935.

Aris, R., *History of Political Thought in Germany from* 1789 *to* 1815, London, 1936.

Black, J. B., *The Art of History*, London, 1926.

Bury, J. B., *The Idea of Progress*, London, 1920.

Butler, E. M., *The Tyranny of Greece over Germany*, Cambridge, 1935

Carr, H. W., *Leibniz*, London, 1928.

Chevrillon, A., *Taine*, 7th edition, Paris, 1932.

Dilthey, W., 'Der entwicklungsgeschichtliche Pantheismus', and 'Das achtzehnte Jahrhundert und die geschichtliche Welt', in *Gesammelte Schriften*, ii and iii, Leipzig and Berlin, 1914, 1927.

Dyboski, R., *Periods of Polish Literary History*, Oxford, 1923.

Fester, R., *Rousseau und die deutsche Geschichtsphilosophie*, Stuttgart, 1890.

Fischel, A., *Der Panslawismus bis zum Weltkrieg*, Berlin, 1919.

Flint, R., *History of the Philosophy of History*, Edinburgh, 1893. Still valuable on Herder; indicates some aspects of his influence as well.

Flöter, A. H. F., *Die Begründung der Geschichtlichkeit der Geschichte in der Philosophie des deutschen Idealismus*, Halle, 1936.

Fueter, E., *Geschichte der neueren Historiographie*, Munich and Berlin, 1911.

Gooch, G. P., *Germany and the French Revolution*, London, 1920. Discusses with authority the reactions of men of letters to the Revolution.

Gundolf, F., *Shakespeare und der deutsche Geist*, Berlin, 1911. A somewhat one-sided chapter on Herder.

Hatfield, H. C., *Winckelmann and his German Critics*, 1755-81, New York, 1943.

Hayes, C. J. H., *Historical Evolution of Modern Nationalism*, New York, 1931.

Haym, R., *Die Romantische Schule*, 5th edition, Berlin, 1928.

Jelinek, H., *Histoire de la littérature tchèque des origines à 1850*, Paris, 1931.

Jolles, M., *Das deutsche Nationalbewußtsein im Zeitalter Napoleons*, Frankfurt a.M., 1936.

Kind, J. L., *Edward Young in Germany*, New York, 1906.

King, B., *Life of Mazzini*, London, 1902.

Korff, H. A., *Geist der Goethezeit*, 2 vols., Leipzig, 1923-30.

Lehmann, M., *Freiherr vom Stein*, Berlin, 1920.

Lempicki, S. von, *Geschichte der deutschen Literaturwissenschaft bis zum Ende des 18. Jahrhunderts*, Göttingen, 1920.

Lempicki, S. von, 'Bücherwelt und wirkliche Welt', *Deutsche Vierteljahrsschrift*, iii, 1925. A useful study of the origins of Romanticism.

Lohre, H., *Von Percy zum Wunderhorn*, Berlin, 1902.

Masaryk, T. G., *The Spirit of Russia*, 2 vols., London, 1919.

Masaryk, T. G., *The Making of a State*, London, 1925. Both these works contain many fruitful references to Herder and his influence.

Mazzini, G., *Life and Writings*, 6 vols., London, 1890-1.

Meinecke, F., *Weltbürgertum und Nationalstaat*, 6th edition, Munich and Berlin, 1922.

Meinecke, F., *Die Entstehung des Historismus*, 2 vols., Munich and Berlin, 1936. Contains an invaluable chapter on Herder and fixes him definitively in his place in the development of historical thought.

Metzke, E., *J. G. Hamanns Stellung in der Philosophie des 18. Jahrhunderts*, Halle, 1934.

Nadler, J., 'Goethe oder Herder?' in *Deutscher Geist, Deutscher Osten*, München, 1937. A very stimulating address.

Oncken, H., 'Deutsche geistige Einflüsse in der europäischen National-bewegung des 19. Jahrhunderts', *Deutsche Vierteljahrsschrift*, vii, 1929.

Price, L. M., *The Reception of English Literature in Germany*, Berkeley, 1932.

Raumer, R. von, *Geschichte der germanischen Philologie*, Munich, 1870.

Rehm, W., *Griechentum und Goethezeit*, Leipzig, 1932.

Robertson, J. G., *Genesis of Romantic Theory*, Cambridge, 1923.

Roth, L., *Spinoza*, London, 1929.

Schultz, F., *Klassik und Romantik der Deutschen*, I, Stuttgart, 1935. Has a useful if discursive chapter on Herder.

Temperley, H. W. V., *History of Serbia*, London, 1919.

Tieghem, P. van, *Le préromantisme*, 2 vols., Paris, 1924–30. A series of invaluable studies on general and special problems in eighteenth-century literature.

Tombo, R., *Ossian in Germany*, New York, 1901.

Troeltsch, E., *Der Historismus und seine Probleme* (*Gesammelte Schriften*, iii), Tübingen, 1922.

Unger, R., *Hamann und die Aufklärung*, 2 vols., Halle, 1925.

Unger, R., *Gesammelte Studien*, 2 vols., Berlin, 1929. Include essays on 'Vom Werden und Wesen der neueren deutschen Literaturwissenschaft', 'Zur Entstehung des Problems der historischen Objektivität bis Hegel', 'Die Vorbereitung der Romantik in der ostpreußischen Literatur des 18. Jahrhunderts', 'Hamann und die Romantik', 'Zur Geschichte des Palinge-nesiegedankens im 18. Jahrhundert', 'Hamann und die Empfindsamkeit', all of them full of suggestion.

Wagener, H. F., *Das Eindringen von Percys Reliques in Deutschland*, Diss. Heidelberg, 1897.

Walzel, O., *Das Prometheussymbol von Shaftesbury zu Goethe*, 2nd edition, Munich, 1932.

Walzel, O., *Deutsche Romantik*, 2 vols., 5th edition, Leipzig and Berlin, 1923.

Weiser, C. F., *Shaftesbury und das deutsche Geistesleben*, Leipzig, 1916.

Wiese, M., *Der sentimentale Mensch*, Stuttgart, 1924.

GENERAL INDEX

INDEX OF REFERENCES TO
HERDER'S WORKS